COMPOSING MUSIC SERIES: VOLUME I

ELEMENTS OF MUSIC COMPOSITION, 3ᴿᴰ EDITION

G000163150

submit@uremusic.com

Printed in the United States of America

First Printing, 2008

Printed Date: 2021, REV. 1

www.uremusic.com

www.kevinure.com

www.themusicalcore.com

Table of Contents

4

Introduction

I've dedicated this book to all of my students over the years who have asked tough questions, which often necessitated the development of improved teaching techniques. Many of the ideas in this text developed as I taught composers through my online studio at UreMusic.com. The 2nd Edition included enhancements in the form of more explanations and details that have emerged through my experience as an instructor at The University of Nevada, Las Vegas. Ultimately, the goal of the text is to provide students with information that I have acquired over the years through my own experiences as an instructor and composer. The 3rd Edition consists of minor edits and formatting changes to make this book easier to use.

The text is not intended to be an instructional manual, though it often serves that purpose. Instead, this is a book provides an introduction to the important concepts I've learned as a composer and instructor. It also serves as a starting point for more advanced work in composition. The *Elements of Music Composition* tackles the thornier questions that arise when learning to compose music in an effort to avoid many of the mistakes that younger composers often make. The *Elements of Music Composition* answers essential questions about the idea of comprehensibility and coherence in music, which stems from the concept of composing organically. In that vein, this book offers more of a philosophy of music composition than a theory. The hope is that composers, musicians, and music-lovers can use this information as a starting point and catalyst for further study.

I published the first edition of this text in 2008 to meet the needs of composers who didn't know where to start with their training. While there were many suitable theory textbooks available on the market, texts that sufficiently dealt with the craft and art of music composition were in short supply and outdated. Composers are often at a loss for where to seek out additional information. While I was trying to learn more about the compositional process, I started to write down many of the ideas that I came across. Eventually, those ideas began to take shape into a philosophy of my own, and this text took form. This text offers a carefully thought-out conversation on the craft of music composition, and it's based on the questions my students have continually asked me over the years.

This book doesn't push or endorse the creation of any one style of music. Many of my tonally bound students often expressed concern that I would make them compose highly dissonant music. While I do tend to write music that is more dissonant, the principles of music composition in this book can be applied very generally across a wide variety of genres. This book also doesn't expect you to write in any particular manner. The concepts apply to many styles of music composition.

Intended Audience

Composers, musicians, and music lovers will find this text informative regardless of their current knowledge of music theory. Those who can read music stand to gain the most from this text, but the majority of readers can benefit from the information contained herein without an extensive background in music. Readers who navigate this book successfully will receive a comprehensive overview of the vital subject areas all composers should master. This text is primarily concept-based and intended to provide a lens for composition students to view the relationships amongst the tenets of music composition. With the *Composing Music* series, it's possible to get a complete education in a method of composition without spending a fortune on school.

The *Elements of Music Composition* caters to composers. Still, the text is equally well-suited to musicians and listeners who want to develop a deeper understanding of musical creation. Throughout this text, I will often speak directly to composers, but understand that the concepts addressed are fundamental to musicians and music lovers as well.

While this text does focus on several basic topics, including dynamics, articulations, motives, rhythm, and melody, the definitions of these concepts are cursory since the text employs them in an advanced manner to show how composers may use these concepts in a musical work. Seemingly disconnected concepts come together to weave a tapestry of information that culminates in the concluding section on composing organic music. The text is designed to be read straight through without the need for students to complete assignments. Advanced concepts are outlined in simple terms throughout the book, and students should aim to dig deeper and research any unfamiliar topics. After reading the *Elements of Music Composition*, readers will be ready to develop their technique with the *Music Composition Technique Builder*.

For the beginning composer: Composers learn about the most important subjects to study. Readers gain an understanding of essential musical concepts, including how to combine elements.

For the advanced composer: A discussion of the aesthetics of music will provide the starting point for combining various techniques and systems into a unified, powerful, and practical approach to composing music in a variety of genres.

For the musician and music lover: Music education tends to teach music students more about the character of music and less about the construction. Teachers often approach music in schools intending to teach spatial reasoning, teamwork, and helping students learn to discuss music in abstract terms. Necessary music skills are usually limited to learning essential note names, instruments, and basic rhythm reading. More advanced programs may also teach basic chords and scales. Teaching only necessary music skills leads to an incomplete understanding and appreciation of music, even if it does help students become acquainted with some basic musical concepts.

An Overview of the Text

If you are advanced, it may be tempting to skip over the first two parts and dive straight into Part III or IV. While you can do this to get a sense of the end goal, it's highly recommended you take the time to absorb the insights in each part. Part I and Part II present the definitions of essential concepts. After accomplishing this, Part III and IV teach composers to join the elements of music cohesively.

The *Elements of Music Composition* offers a glimpse into the process of integrating the concepts studied in the core subjects to create more effective compositions. Core subjects typically include harmony, counterpoint, theory, orchestration, and form. Student composers typically learn these concepts separately. This practice provides mixed results with only the most talented musical minds understanding the connections among the separate disciplines.

Using the study of orchestration as an example, each instrument group serves a vital function in the performance of a musical work. However, while orchestration teaches how different combinations of instruments can be used to create a desired *coloring* of the music, it fails to address the concept of how the study of orchestration also relates to the motivic, melodic, and harmonic elements of a musical work. Composers need a method that teaches the core subjects in a way that can also be related to other areas of composition instruction.

Teaching core subjects in an integrated and organized sequence proves to be a challenge for even the most experienced teachers. With the right organization and presentation, a student composer could begin to understand how the tenets of music composition are related. Since the most widely used systems teach these subjects separately, the composer must typically rely on instinct, talent, training, and technique. Fortunate composers can also study with a highly experienced and qualified composer who is also a creative pedagogue. Even then, studying with a composer doesn't guarantee that the composer will learn the concept of coherence and how core subjects relate to each other.

When a composer learns the core subjects separately, they rarely receive instruction on how to employ these broad concepts in an integrated manner. However, absent a more complete and integrated method to teach composers these techniques, it makes sense to compartmentalize these subjects at first and let the student composer know that the merging of concepts into an artform must occur at a later time. Once the student has learned the fundamentals, the student can then unhinge the 'tethers of instruction' or 'withering soul trapped in purgatory' to develop a personal style.

Self-motivated composers who can think creatively and apply broad, abstract principles to their training will benefit most from this text. The concepts in this text lay the groundwork for a complete, flexible, and unified philosophy of music composition. As a primer, this text gives context to the tenets of music composition so that students can view the bigger picture when studying these independent subjects. As intended, this text may raise more questions than it answers. Still, these questions will illuminate a path to composing music that is richly rewarding, highly flexible, based on sound principles, and intuitive.

Some of the concepts in this book may seem to fly in the face of some traditional music theory instruction, but this misunderstanding is often due to a lack of knowledge. College courses begin with simplified traditional harmony. The techniques employed are often suitable only for chorale writing. Learning music theory that stems from composers like Bach, Haydn, Mozart, and Beethoven creates composers who write in the style of these masters. In contrast, revealing the underlying compositional process creates students who can think like composers. In this way, students can learn to think about musical development and create original and compelling artistic works.

Preparatory Work

For students who need instruction in the basics of music, *The Musical Core* provides a complete entry-level program with online quizzes and ear training exercises that begins with note names and ends with identifying scales and key signatures. If any of the concepts in this book are confusing or complicated, *The Musical Core* offers an excellent starting point.

Book Organization

This book is divided into four parts to organize the content and make it easier for you to process and learn the concepts in this text. This book is designed to function as a self-teaching manual or as supplemental material in private lessons or courses. Many concepts are repeated, which eliminates the need for cross-referencing throughout the textbook. In order for each part to stand on its own, earlier concepts are repeated and expounded upon in an additive manner.

Part I: Composing Original Music is designed to introduce the concept of composing music as a lifelong craft and discuss the importance of composing as both craft and art. This part also deals with the issue of motivation and gives some advice for creating a composing schedule.

Part II: Systems of Music Composition gives an overview of opposing systems – one tonal and one atonal. Composers have used these systems to compose music over the years. This section introduces the possibility of creating an original system of musical composition. The goal of this text is to provide a framework for creating an individual and unique system for editing a composition. This goal can be best demonstrated through the use of highly established systems that are already fleshed out.

Part III: Elements, Motives, and Cornerstones deals with the essential components of music that composers historically study to achieve mastery of the craft. Elements and cornerstones of music are critical to developing coherent music. The elements section serves a primarily instructional purpose. The cornerstones section deals with complex concepts beyond the scope of this text, so only a brief explanation of each cornerstone (core subject) is discussed. Ideally, readers learn about each cornerstone, and then put in the work to study these cornerstones in-depth with the knowledge of how they relate to the elements in a musical work. It would be unrealistic to expect any single book to discuss each cornerstone in detail.

Part IV: Organic Music serves as a condensed summary of this book, and it provides additional details on the concepts of coherence and comprehensibility.

These basic concepts lead readers on a path toward understanding how the often-separate elements of music composition integrate into a single theory. Organicism is a philosophy that explores the connections between music of the past and modern music. Consider Part IV as a recapitulation of the text that brings about information from the opening chapters to summarize and bring the discussion to a close.

PART I: COMPOSING MUSIC

THE PHILOSOPHY OF ORGANICISM

Traditionally, there are three basic premises that describe the philosophy of organicism.

1. The whole is more than the sum of its parts.
2. A quality of wholeness is present in every detail of the work.
3. An alteration in part is an alteration in the whole.

Composers who apply the concepts of organicism to their works don't always agree on how organicism should be applied. This makes the concept of organicism fluid and flexible as a system for thinking about musical compositions.

The concept of organicism was prominent in the Romantic period, unfortunately, it also later appealed to the Nazis. The association with the Nazis made the concept of organicism unpalatable, and it faded into the background as an outdated, and even dangerous, way of thinking about music and art. Science and empirically based theories took its place.

Plato is one of the earliest philosophers to accept the concept of organicism. The philosophy rejects the idea that the smaller parts in a musical work solely dictate the function of the larger components. Instead of insisting that the smallest musical ideas determine the larger formal functions in a musical work, organicism insists that small musical ideas are both created by and create the larger formal structures. All of the parts in an artistic work function in a symbiotic relationship. Thought of in this way, it wouldn't be possible to have a form that wasn't influenced by its smaller motives and vice-versa.

Sentence Structure - Mozart, Rondo in D, K. 485, mm. 9-16

Reflecting upon the various time periods in music demonstrates the progression of organicism. The sentence structure is a type of phrase that consists of two repeated basic ideas followed by a continuation of those ideas in a presentation-continuation structure. There must also be a lack of strong cadence between the presentation and continuation phrases. The concept of sentence structure can help better illuminate the concept of organicism. The presentation function of a sentence structure provides the opening material in the form of melodic and motive content that sets the stage for further development. The melodic-motivic content is then fragmented and liquidated in the continuation portion of the phrase.

While a complete discussion of sentence structure is not required for understanding concepts in this text, an example should help to demonstrate a point. In Mozart's *Rondo in D*, there is a clear example of sentence structure. Measures 9 and 10 introduce a basic idea that is then repeated in measures 11 and 12. The first four-measure presentation phrase does not conclude with a cadence before moving on to the continuation phrase in measure 13. If you lack the theory knowledge to identify a cadence, you should listen to the piece to hear how the phrase in measures 9 to 12 feels as if it must continue to the continuation phrase in measure 13. In measure 13, the basic idea is now broken down and fragmented. The rate of harmonic change increases and the overall rhythmic activity increases as well.

14

In the Classical period, the unification of motives to form the overall larger structures would be limited to the development of the phrase. This opening motive would likely have no bearing on the development of later sections in the work, and opening motives will rarely dictate the form of a piece. It was the Romantic period that began to take the concept of a motive and apply it more comprehensively to determine the manner that a piece would progress. However, on the surface level, the opening basic idea does repeat to create coherence in the piece, and it is later fragmented and broken-apart to create the continuation portion of the phrase. Music often uses the concept of a basic idea to create the structure for individual phrases, sections, movements, and entire works. During and after the Romantic period, it became not just about creating a phrase that was built from a single unifying motive or basic idea; composers started using simple motives to also create the large-scale structure for an entire work.

In essence, a composer who composes organically believes that you can't have a musical form without a melody, and you can't have a melody without a musical form. The large and small musical ideas feed off each other and need each other to exist.

Compound Melody

One technique a composer often employs involves a concept known as a compound melody. Using this technique, a seemingly innocuous series of chords may reveal multiple independent melodies hidden inside a chord progression. (A chord progression uses *a series of chords that progress toward a harmonic goal*. A chord progression differs from a chord succession since a succession uses a *series of chords with no harmonic goal*.) The performer who misses these details tends to misinterpret a musical work.

Compound melody is especially common in the Classical and Romantic periods. Using the Mozart example again, compound melody can be seen in the left-hand piano part. The reduction shown above the Mozart excerpt shows how the left-hand piano part can be separated into three stepwise melodies. This is a common technique that is used in the Classical and Romantic period. The technique also transfers over into 20th and 21st century music.

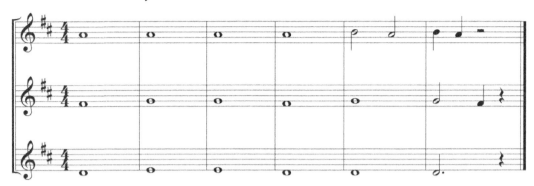

Notice how the left-hand piano part can be separated into two lines. The reduction does not deal with the melody, though the A in measure 9, the G in measure 10 and the A in measure 12 can be considered to be another form of compound melody. Additionally, notice how the F on beat 3 of measure 9, the E on the offbeat of 2, and the F on the offbeat of 12 also serve a form of compound melody. Especially in the Classical period, these stepwise lines can be seen throughout a musical work.

Organicism in Music

A simple way to think about organicism is to relate it to the human body. The body consists of several organs and body parts. We recognize these parts as belonging to the whole, but no single part is required to make a human. Lose an arm or leg, and the rest of the body can still function and be identifiable as belonging to a human being. The same concept can be applied to music that is composed organically.

Every part of a musical work should serve some vital role but removing a part doesn't prevent the work from functioning.

Arnold Schoenberg was a famous composer and theorist in his time, and this text is partially based on his unfinished theory of coherence. After writing the first edition of this text, I discovered some of his lesser-known notes and documents that describe a theory of coherence that he was never able to complete. I studied many of his drafts and used those to reinforce concepts in this book. While I don't agree with all of his ideas, his writings helped to support the concepts in this text.

Schoenberg believed in two parts of the philosophy of organicism:

- The whole is more than the sum of its parts
- A quality of wholeness is present in every detail of the work.

He disagrees with the premise that alterations in any part require alterations to the entire work. I tend to agree with this as well, since losing an arm doesn't mean that your other arm doesn't function, or you cease to be human. Losing a single part may affect functionality, but it doesn't mean the entire composition has to be rewritten.

Consider the concept of a chain reaction. In a mechanical process, the action of one part creates a response in a cause-and-effect relationship. This causal relationship is apparent when you start a car. After turning the key, a series of systems engage, and the vehicle starts running. Release the brake pedal and press on the gas, and the car starts moving forward. Many composers create music in this way, and it is a perfectly valid method. A motive is divined, and then the motive creates every other aspect of the work. While this is a method discussed extensively in this book, writing an organic work needs to incorporate more relationships than simple cause and effect.

In an organic process, the parts serve a relationship to the entire work. The effect is not causal. Consider a symphonic work with a first and second theme. If the work is created using a causal series of relationships, the first theme would create the second theme; however, this isn't how most music is composed. The first theme typically doesn't cause the second theme to appear; they both serve a relationship to the entire work and serve to create variation and development. Composers can present an idea in several ways without altering the essence of the composition, provided the alterations agree with the nature of the organism. Furthermore, in an organic composition, the larger structure needs to be intimately connected to the motive. In this way motives, elements, and cornerstones grow and change together.

Composing Original Music

A discussion of the role of music theory, creating a composition routine, and dealing with motivational issues offers musicians the chance to plan and implement a schedule that works.

> *The moment when one is composing music is not the time to recall the rules that might hold our genius in bondage. We must have recourse to the rules only when our genius and our ear seem to deny what we are seeking.*
>
> *We may note that the semiskilled generally use a chord because it is familiar to them or pleases them, but the expert uses it only to the extent that he feels its power.*
>
> *It is often by seeing and hearing musical works (operas and other good musical compositions), rather than by rules, that taste is formed.*
>
> *~ Jean Philippe Rameau*
>
> *from La Noveau système de musique thèorique, 1726.*

Jean Philippe Rameau was responsible for creating the first complete music theory treatise. While aspects of theory were present before he came onto the scene, he was the first theorist to organize our modern conception of chord construction and progressions into a single text. Despite being one of the early modern theorists, he still advocates for composers to use their ears before resorting to rules.

Without formal training in music and exposure to the works of established composers, the ability to accurately judge the originality of music is severely limited. Musicians, composers, and music lovers need adequate musical training to assess new musical works intelligently; however, the level of musical training required depends mainly on the goals of the individual. A casual music-lover won't need the same level of musical understanding as an orchestral composer who aims to push the field of music composition to new heights. Musical training may mean different things for a composer, musician, or listener. However, most people can instinctually tell the difference between an artfully crafted work and one that is derivative. Theory knowledge is critical for identifying derivative works, and it serves as a starting point for composing original works.

Composers: Composers need advanced musical training to create original works that are original and not derivative. Proper musical training not only teaches composers to create music, but it also refines the ear and develops an intuition for music. By learning the techniques and theories of the past, the modern composer is better prepared to compose new music. In a sense, studying music, traditionally through harmony and counterpoint, offers a way for modern composers to take private lessons with Bach, Haydn, Mozart, Brahms, Beethoven, and many of the great composers of the past. A composer that creates derivative works exists somewhere between a composer and arranger.

Musicians: Musicians need formal training to learn how to play in multiple styles, interpret the aims of a composer, and gain an in-depth understanding of the composer's goals. When a musician doesn't understand how a composer thinks, they are at a significant disadvantage. A performance may lack nuance, or the performer may miss some crucial cue that would dramatically change the interpretation of a work.

Listeners: Audience members and casual listeners with formal knowledge of the basics can connect and form more profound, lasting connections with the music they already love. Knowing the methods used by many composers to create music can help the listener to find hidden melodies and messages within a musical work. The astute listener can walk away from a performance with an informed opinion of the musical work. A greater understanding of the elements of music composition can open the door to new music they didn't previously enjoy.

Composers who aim to compose music quickly can "steal" from the masters of the past to create "fast food" music designed for casual consumption. Music composed with strict adherence to theory creates logical and effective music, but it doesn't result in a truly original work. Works that borrow from other composers' techniques don't tell a unique harmonic story. When the message of the lyrics or the passion of the singer is more important than the notes, "fast food" accessible music can serve a vital

20

role since it's great to enjoy a musical work with a fun message and an exciting rhythm. However, even the most accessible music can benefit from employing compositional techniques to give a piece more substance and make the musical work entertaining for years to come.

There is nothing inherently wrong with imitating the masters of the past and creating a sort of hybrid profession that blurs the line between composer and arranger. Though, it is important to understand the difference. Arrangers rely on reconstructing the harmonies of composers who came before in creative and novel ways. Composers learn from the past to create something new. Composers, arrangers and hybrids all have their place in music.

The Tenets of Music Composition

Composers traditionally receive instruction in the five tenets of music composition, which include form, counterpoint, instrumentation, orchestration, and theory. Throughout the text, these subjects are referred to as tenets, foundations, disciplines, and core subjects. An attempt is made to define these concepts, but this is not intended to be a complete course in musicianship. Therefore, it's unrealistic to expect that a single book can teach form, counterpoint, instrumentation, orchestration, and theory. Several excellent books teach these subjects comprehensively and separately. This text is the bridge that is designed to both introduce these concepts to younger composers and set advanced composers on a path toward combining the tenets into an integrated craft of music composition.

The Role of Music Theory

Music theory is often the bane of all undergraduate music majors. It's the subject that seems to be the biggest impediment to the student's life, especially when ensembles and instrumental techniques are vying for the student's attention. Ask a music student how they feel about the music theory courses they are taking, and the answer may come as a horrified glance. The undergraduate trying to balance a schedule made up wholly of one- and two-credit courses is not merely taking music theory; they are trying to survive its onslaught.

Humor aside, music theory is often pushed to the bottom of the list of priorities. This truth tends to prevail, whether a musician studies formally or independently with or without the support of an institution. As tricky as music theory may seem for many musicians, the alternative to learning about the composers of the past is far more taxing. Music theory offers a shortcut to understanding centuries worth of musical development. Musicians can learn by performing, listening, and analyzing a mountain of musical works, or they can use theory to summarize the most important developments in music.

22

Music theory doesn't necessarily produce perfectly crafted music, but keep in mind the objective of music composition. Composers have written music over the centuries to engage and entertain audiences. Since the audience is ultimately the judge, composers tend to focus on the techniques that are well-received and actively avoid the techniques that fail.

When a composition is not well-received, composers tend to learn from their mistakes and try again. If a piece succeeds, the composer takes note and tries to replicate that success. In this way, new composers learn from listening and absorbing the music of the past and intuitively employ the most successful techniques. More advanced composers do the same thing, but they turn intuition into practical knowledge and uncover the theories behind a work to push the field of composition forward. Music theory is not just a set of rules, but a summary of the techniques that the most successful composers have employed over the years.

Music belongs to the people who listen. Without people to perceive and enjoy musical works, you can't have emotion in music, which means composers must learn to combine knowledge with intuition to create lasting works.

There is a strange cultural phenomenon that pits knowledge against ignorance, which results in the creation of an inside-outside culture. Those who are knowledgeable of past works may view a derivative composition as cliché and uninspired, which can bar entry to a wider array of music. Those who are less informed may fall in love with the work, but never realize that a composition is derivative. The result is that the listener never realizes that the music they love is a reproduction of another composer's music. Both extremes have their drawbacks, but the uninformed composer never truly understands the music they are writing and how it is constructed. Lack of knowledge puts the uninformed composer into a mysterious fog where music is created solely by intuition, which results in a lack of intention.

While the progenitor doesn't always produce the most polished version of a style, it's still useful to know the origins of a composer's music. When the composer who created the style remains unknown to the listener, it leaves an unfortunate gap in the listener's understanding and appreciation of music. Studying music theory can teach a composer, performer, or listener about the myriad techniques used in the creation and development of musical works.

For illustrative purposes, imagine a composer creates a new work using a scale built entirely on whole tones without realizing the scale already exists. Or, perhaps the composer knows the whole tone scale is a scale built entirely on whole steps but doesn't grasp the underlying structural principles that made the technique work effectively. With fervor and anticipation of great music to come, the composer creates several pieces using the two versions of the whole tone scale. After years of writing musical works based on whole tones, the composer realizes how the problems of the whole tone scale were primarily worked out by composers who spent their lives manipulating these scales for musical purposes. It's a tragic tale since these solutions were available to review and documented by music theorists in summary form.

Instead of spending those years reinventing the wheel, the composer could have taken a few hours to learn about the structural function of these scales. At which point, the composer could then get some practical application by listening to music created using those techniques to see how concepts were realized in music. This information could lead to discoveries and insights, and the composer may even decide to move on to more modern scales such as the octatonic scale. The composer still benefits from the time thinking about and composing music, but valuable time was spent working through musical problems that were already well-documented rather than taking the technique to new vistas. With so many techniques available to composers, it would be hard to learn them all in a lifetime. Theory provides a baseline so that composers don't have to start from scratch.

Consider the composer who loves birdsong. Perhaps they begin transcribing bird songs heard in the wild. The composer could save time and work more efficiently by studying other composers who also composed birdsong and used it in their works. If the composer knew that Messiaen spent a lifetime notating various bird calls with extreme accuracy, the birdsong-loving composer would know that studying Messiaen's music would provide an invaluable starting point. The knowledgeable composer would also realize that because our western scales are tempered and don't conform perfectly to the natural overtones in nature, it's impossible to notate birdsong precisely without bending a few pitches. A knowledge of instrumentation would provide the necessary techniques to accomplish this on appropriate instruments.

Experimenting with ideas and arriving at the same realizations as other composers isn't a waste of time as an intellectual and problem-solving exercise; however, benefitting from one's predecessors can move the process of composing new music along more efficiently. The energy spent problem-solving can be applied to the development of new ideas.

Some composers expend their efforts trying to prove music theory wrong, but this completely misses the point. Music theory isn't a law of music; it only provides theories based on the trends of past composers. Ignoring the goldmine that is music theory discounts more than a single idea, textbook, or musical period. Theory summarizes centuries of combined knowledge and progress in music and represents the intuitive principles of music that have developed throughout the centuries. Even if a successful performer or musician doesn't understand music theory, in many ways, it's imprinted on our musical minds since most music has logic and tendencies. The real question is not whether music theory is useful; it's whether a musician can afford to ignore centuries of insight into principles that have helped composers create compelling musical works.

Writing an original composition requires the composer to understand existing music theory to discover what already exists quickly. Composers must seek out the music of other composers to digest, learn, and push the art of music composition forward. Listening to music with a score in hand offers an excellent tool for a composer who is learning, but it's even better if the composer can compare the similarities in the work to other composers. Theory takes what is common among a group of composers and explains it in an easily digestible format.

Becoming a Composer

The ability to mentally envision an entire work is a lofty goal for composers, and it is a skill that can be developed and taught. The secret to creating phenomenal musical works lies in the human ability to imagine vivid internal worlds and bring them into reality. Once a composition can be fully imagined in the mind, the next steps require the ability to notate your ideas so that you can employ comprehensive compositional practices and effectively realize your ideas.

Many composers have forgotten the most basic principle of composing a new musical work – it's critical to develop the inner ear above all other theories and techniques. When I was younger, I did not have the ability to mentally envision my compositions. Now that I do, I'm much freer in my ability to compose new musical worlds. As valuable as it is to hear your compositions without an external music source, the inner ear is most important while creating the initial composition. *Composers still need theory to learn about what already exists.*

While working on technique, it's a good idea to become acquainted with some of the basics of music composition. These concepts help prepare you for advanced study in music composition and highlight the most critical components of the craft. Composers must also develop a highly refined ear that is capable of identifying intervals and chords quickly. Otherwise, the composer becomes limited by their mental faculties. Composers can develop technique and craft at the same time since these two disciplines can be easily compartmentalized. There is nothing more frustrating than developing the ability to hear a composition entirely in your mind and not having the skills to extract the music and notate it on paper. The next volume of this series discusses how to accomplish this goal.

Understanding how all of the individual aspects of music can, directly and indirectly, influence each other provides the first step in learning how to integrate disparate components. Achieving this goal takes time. Composers must first learn the tenets of music composition. After mastering these subjects, the composer then works toward the creation of original musical works with a greater understanding of how music functions. The process of developing this knowledge can take years of study, and even the most talented composer needs to learn some musical basics to succeed in crafting artful musical works.

The path to becoming a composer is not an easy one, but by investing the time to make daily progress, composing can be extremely fulfilling. But, don't take my word for it. Mozart's piano playing was remarkably effortless, and when asked about it, he responded by saying that he worked hard early so that it would be easy later. Composers should take the same approach to learn the tenets of music composition so that this knowledge becomes embedded and accessed effortlessly.

Perhaps Arnold Schoenberg puts it best in his text, *The Musical Idea and Its Presentation:*

> *"At present the theory of harmony [music theory], counterpoint, and the theory of form mainly serve pedagogical purposes. With the possible exception of the theory of harmony, the individual disciplines lack even a truly theoretical basis emanating from other external criteria. On the whole, the consequence is that three different disciplines, which together should constitute the theory of composition, in reality fall apart because they lack a common point of view."*

I should note that Schoenberg considers the tenets of music composition to include only theory, counterpoint, and form; however, I've expanded this definition to include instrumentation and orchestration. Regardless, many attempts have been made to consolidate the tenets of music composition, but they always seem to fall short. The *Elements of Music Composition* aims to provide a common point of view that is useful for linking these disciplines together. For a point of view to work with the massive ideas found within the tenets, it's critical to make that point of view flexible, straightforward, and broadly applicable.

If you're a beginning composer, start by reading through this text and then continue on to the *Music Composition Technique Builder*. At the same time, you should begin studying instrumentation, orchestration, and form. Once you finish the *Music Composition Technique Builder*, you can start the *Craft of Music Composition* series. This series will provide you with a complete undergraduate education in music theory as it relates to a composer. Composers need more than theory; they have to absorb theoretical concepts so that they become second nature. The *Music Composition Technique Builder* sets the stage for this, and the *Craft of Music Composition* takes the skills learned in the *Music Composition Technique Builder* to the next stage.

The Challenge of Composing

Composers must overcome challenges and obstacles in the quest to solve musical problems. Perseverance and work usually results in a solution that manifests itself during more idle hours. Working consistently serves as one of the most valuable insights to learn as a composer. Don't merely compose a piece and then move on to the next one. Work daily and try to see the different sides and characters of the motives and melodies in a new work. Concentrated effort has a tendency to result in rewards in the form of profound revelations about your musical works.

Learning the craft of music composition should prove challenging. If no obstacles present themselves, then it might be necessary to go deeper and think more intently about the music. It's a cliché, but most things worth having require work, so commit now to finishing this text and starting your journey to become a more successful composer. Even if it takes years to master the tenets of music composition, you owe it to yourself to discover everything that you are capable of achieving.

Many of my private students have revealed the fear that they can't compose music, but they have a strong desire to learn. They worry that they don't have the talent necessary to create melodies and build a complete and cohesive musical work. Usually, the problem is that they are trying to write a symphony or a masterpiece with every new piece. Composing is a process, and not every piece is going to be brilliant. Believing you can't do something gets in the way of working, and it's usually not based in reality. Push this kind of talk aside. I have yet to meet a student who couldn't be taught to compose music – at least on a purely mechanical level.

It's perfectly normal and expected to feel doubtful about your abilities. It's common to second-guess your choice to study music composition, but it's important that you don't quit if composing is in your blood. Push forward and keep working. Keep in mind that success in the field may not come exactly in the way you envision, but you can have a career in music if you are willing to stay committed and keep your eye on the goal even during tough times.

Changes in technique and ability may manifest as leaps of insight, but they seem to be accompanied more often by a fall into the abyss of confusion and doubt. The development of a composer is not a straight line from novice to master. In my experience, it is during the times of most considerable doubt and insecurity that you learn the most important lessons. Keep studying and work through these tough times, and you'll find your way to the other side with new revelations and greater confidence.

Expect and embrace the dips and valleys along the path to becoming a successful composer. Expect to get worse before you improve. Then, expect to improve and then get worse. Breakthroughs generally come with a moment of clarity where you suddenly see things from a completely different perspective. At first, a breakthrough tends to be exciting. However, you may eventually find yourself yearning for the days of ignorance. A breakthrough often makes composing more complicated than it was before.

Techniques that help you compose established styles of music quickly tend to make you good at arranging other composers' ideas. Commit to learning to solve compositional problems and creating original works. Avoid creating works based on pre-constructed theories, techniques, or chord tables. By all means, learn theory, but do it so that you can create music that is genuinely original and unique.

Ultimately, composing music can be highly rewarding for yourself, your friends, and your family. Even if you never gain recognition, the work you put in can become a part of your legacy. Composition can be a lifelong hobby that you will never outgrow. There will always be new riddles to solve and new ideas to present in their best form possible. Remember that composing isn't just about creating an enjoyable or catchy melody. The act of composing is part craft and part art. You need to have the art to create enjoyable melodies, and you need the craft to realize your ideas in the most elegant way.

Rate of Progress

No quick fixes or magic pills exist that turn you into Beethoven in an hour. Composers and theorists who want to make a quick buck sell you courses that promise to make you an instant composer or learn to create symphonies with one simple trick. If you want to write compelling music, you're going to have to put in some serious hours. Find time each day to make progress, even if your progress is slow.

If you become impatient, remind yourself of the following:
1. Quick fixes almost always result in long-term deficiencies, and you'll spend more time trying to fix simple mistakes than if you learned from the masters of the past.
2. A little work daily produces a mountain of work over a lifetime. You may often find yourself thinking that you can start tomorrow, but tomorrow often gets delayed.
3. Time and effort directed at a task are often proportional to quality. But often, you need to take a break, do something relaxing and come back to the task the next hour or day.

Be patient. Nobody became a composer or musician overnight. Even Mozart was trained relentlessly as a child and given extensive instruction by his father. Music composition is about getting to know your music, connecting with your inner resources, and representing your work in the most elegant way. There are often numerous ways to solve a compositional problem, but the difference between a mediocre and a great composer often comes down to how they solve problems and present their work.

While there is something satisfying about completing a work quickly and hearing it performed, imagine the satisfaction that results from knowing you explored every avenue and intimate detail of your musical work. Put in the energy required to complete your next musical work effectively. Expending the right level of energy gives you the confidence to put that work aside and begin working on your next composition. Not only that, but you develop more considerable skills and techniques to help you write your next piece.

As you learn, your old compositions may seem immature, but remember, they serve as a marker that shows you how you have progressed. Even though I'm a victim of revisiting my older works to improve upon them, it's generally more productive to leave those works in the past and move on to new compositions once they are finished. If your new compositions show more nuance and a more refined style, that's fine. It doesn't mean you have to go back in time to try to fix older compositions. Composers are known for having reasonably defined musical periods in their life, and your early pieces may demonstrate an early period in your compositions.

Historians typically break up Beethoven's career into three periods. Other composers exhibit similar developments with an early, middle, and late period of music composition. The only restriction that I would suggest you put on yourself is to avoid releasing a recording of your music or publishing your music until you have put in the time to master the tenets of music composition. Master composers of the past published their works only after completing a complete course of study. If you wait, at least you'll know that when you published your compositions, you had a firm grasp of the tenets of music composition, and any perceived shortcomings were not the result of poor education.

With time, your old beliefs about what it means to be a composer may drop away, and it may feel like you're starting all over again. As you develop, what once seemed like a great accomplishment begins to seem amateurish. Every time you think you're about to cross over the hill and reach a resting point, you'll find another more massive hill looming. The truth is that I don't know a single good composer who feels they have reached a point where further development is no longer needed.

The ebb and flow of progress is both the challenge and the joy of becoming a composer. In your time on Earth, you could never learn everything you need to know about music to feel satisfied with your craft. The unsurmountable quest for learning is what makes composing at once thrilling and frustrating. Composing provides you with a continual challenge that entertains and engages you by posing problems and challenges to solve for the rest of your life.

I'm going to extreme lengths to talk about the difficulties inherent in learning to compose music for one fundamental reason:

I don't want you to give up on your dream of becoming a composer.

After teaching composers for decades, I have come to the belief that anybody with a desire to compose can get satisfying results. However, it's not going to be comfortable, and you have to work. Composing is hard work. Your rate of progress doesn't matter as long as you continue to develop and keep writing. Writing every day is the best way to improve as a composer.

The Composition Routine

Many composers work on strict schedules to ensure they stay productive and motivated. Working at the same time each day primes the brain for composition work. There are also composers who refuse to use a schedule. These composers insist that a schedule hampers their work, and it puts them into a limited way of thinking that reduces creativity.

I recommend a compromise: Schedule your technique and formal training, but let your creative work come to you when you're in the right mood. By scheduling your technique and formal training, you will be more likely to develop and improve over time.

Philip Glass has stated that he doesn't worry about inspiration because he makes inspiration come to him. If he gets an idea for a piece during non-work hours, he ignores it unless he is in a composing session. He believes that this enables him to maintain a high level of productivity because his mind has become wired to tune into musical thoughts during specific hours. There is quite a bit of logic to this idea, and it may be something you wish to try.

If you sit down at the same time every day to compose, your mind becomes more creative during that time. Musical ideas tend come to you at your designated hour, which can make the composing hour more effective over time. However, it's also important to keep in mind that Philip Glass is a highly trained composer. If you haven't yet developed the ability to hear music internally, I would suggest that you don't ignore musical ideas that come to you during the day. Don't rush to write them down, just take a moment to listen and try to develop your ability to hear those ideas in greater detail. Listening to music in your mind throughout the day can help you to develop your inner ear. I still recommend that you sit down at specific times to notate those ideas but let them come to you freely and don't try to push all of your musical thoughts into your composing hour.

Personally, I recommend setting up time for a daily routine so that you can continually improve every day, but your own personality and needs may dictate what your routine looks like.

Mozart spaced his composing sessions out throughout the day, and we was essentially composing and practicing his craft consistently. He interspersed his daily work with everyday activities like hanging out with friends, eating, drinking, and putting on concerts (right, everyday events like concerts.) He was often up early in the morning and went to bed late at night. His schedule could be considered random and undisciplined, but he was one of the most prolific composers in history. Many people also don't realize that Mozart didn't just compose music. He was also semi-active as an instructor, and he worked all sorts of odd jobs to maintain his composing habit. An erratic schedule of composing worked for Mozart, but it could be argued that he was composing all the time.

Haydn maintained a consistent practice routine; the following is an excerpt from Griesinger's Biographische Notizen:

> *I would sit down and begin to compose, whether my spirits were sad or happy, serious or playful. Once I had captured an idea, I strove with all my might to develop and sustain it in conformity with the rules of art. In this way I tried to help myself, and this is where so many of our newer composers fall short: they string together one little piece onto another and break off when they have scarcely started. Nothing remains in one's heart after one has listened to such compositions.*

> *I was never a quick writer and always composed with care and diligence. Such works are lasting, however, and the connoisseur knows this immediately from the score. When Cherubini would look over some of my manuscripts, he would always recognize those parts that deserved special marks of distinction.*

> *There was no one near me to confuse or torment me, thus I was obliged to be original.*

Creating a daily routine is essential to developing as a musician. To be clear, once you achieve basic mastery of your craft, the routine becomes less essential. The daily routine relieves some of the anxiety that often comes from being a composer since it allows you the knowledge that you are consistently working toward your goal of being a more flexible and skilled artist. Daily work makes you very good at creating original music. Competence through your daily practice makes you a more effective composer overall.

A routine gets you in the habit of composing every day, which helps you learn that your mood does not dictate whether or not you have the ability to write. Your skills are what make you a composer, and inspiration doesn't always grace us with its presence. Even if your time is spent editing an existing composition and nothing new is created during your composing hour, this is still part of the composing process. Don't underestimate the power of editing; it plays a massive role in the creation of music.

PART II: MUSICAL SYSTEMS
COMPOSING WITH A SYSTEM

Systems of music composition can provide a method for composing within a framework. Mistakes can be avoided, and composers can learn the best practices of the composers of the past. Systems are useful for the purpose of training, but the system can be thrown to the wayside once a student learns the purpose and techniques of a system. Learning how to use the various systems in place will make you a better-educated and more well-rounded composer, but they can only teach you what already exists. It's important to think creatively and discover new ways to present your music.

"The most conspicuous misconception in our educational method is that composers can be fabricated by training. If you go through two years of Harmony, one of Counterpoint, fulfill your requirements in Composition I and Composition II, have some courses in Orchestration and Form, throw in some minor courses for credits, and do some so-called "free" work in a post-graduate course, you are inevitably a composer, because you paid for your courses–or somebody else did–and you can expect to get something for your money. We produce composers the democratic way, as we produce congressmen....

It is extremely dishonest to give every student the education that is meant to turn out a Beethoven, while we know that he will never be more than a medium-sized commonplace composer. Would it not be better, more honest, and even more economical, to provide him with an all-round technique of general validity, on which his talents may thrive.... Trained in this old and renewed system–if the most natural musical activity can be called a system–composers would again be musicians, who could be used in many fields of music equally well..." ~Paul Hindemith in The Composer's Education

Systems of Music Composition

Music theorists have made invaluable efforts to create systems of music composition based on the most successful and representative composers and works from the literature. While these efforts are useful, the theorist can fall prey to a belief in the superiority of music theory. When theory becomes a barometer for judging new works, the art and evolution of music suffers.

Knowledge of music theory is essential to understanding the conventions of the past; however, the accomplishments of a composer who lived in a different economic, social, and political climate should not dictate the rules of art for future generations. Music of the past serves as a guide for writing music that is effective and successful, but it's important to remember that theory is typically the study of the most successful composers and their common techniques. An understanding of the music of the past is essential to developing a profound and well-rounded technique, but music theory must draw the line at dictating what is pleasing and acceptable in music. Theory can only dictate what is most common within narrowly defined boundaries, such as music of a particular composer, time period, style, or musical movement.

Developing an aesthetics of music for composing original works based on general principles and avoiding a strict implementation of rules offers a better path for the composer. Rather than relying on music theory or a system to compose music, it's much more honest to use the skills obtained from studying music theory to instill an understanding and appreciation for the music of the past. At first, this may seem like a contradiction to previous statements in this text. However, a distinction must be made between learning music theory for the sake of building upon the successes of past composers to benefit from their knowledge and learning music theory to continue an antiquated tradition.

Music theory and systems of composition serve the composer by accelerating formal training through the emulation of masterworks. Composers who wish to create original music must eventually forge their own path and trust their instincts, but this can't be accomplished until a composer has a solid understanding of what already exists. Young composers may use systems to bolster a work, create a name, and potentially win a music composition contest, but a composer should guard against absorbing the guidelines of music theory as doctrine.

Music theory serves as training wheels while the composer fleshes out their style and improves their technique for composing sound musical works. When the composer develops the ability to imagine a work from start to finish, the same systems that propped up the apprentice composer become a crutch that serves to hamper true artistic expression. It's at this point the composer must be bold enough to emphatically state that the system of music theory that was instrumental in developing their technique must be further developed to branch out onto an original path.

Systems help composers and musicians complete a crash course in stylistic composition, but these systems are only training wheels to get started. The process of learning to compose is not unlike learning to ride a bike. Training wheels provide the support and balance needed to avoid tumbling to the ground. When the parent suggests removing the wheels, the child may not see the point. For the inexperienced child, it makes little sense to remove such a device that is obviously intended to make it easier (and safer) to ride the bike. If the child fails without the training wheels, the belief that the wheels were needed may get reinforced.

After some practice, the training wheels are removed, and the child learns to keep the bike upright without the added support. The ride may seem stilted and rough at first. Quickly, the fear turns to exhilaration as the rider gains increasing control over the bicycle. Free of the limitations imposed by the training wheels but infused by the skill gained from the initial support, it's possible to ride over an increasing variety of terrain and discover new pathways. This newfound freedom makes the risk associated with falling worthwhile. The beginning composer who fails to move past the conventions of the past gets placed in the same position as the child who refuses to let go of a system that has prevented injury.

Some composers justify their works not on the merits of their own understanding, but on the proper application of a theoretical rule. However, it's also problematic to take the exact opposite approach and refuse to learn anything about musical theories.

These composers don't see the value of any type of formal training and believe they can't be taught anything useful. I might agree that an original approach is best if I ever came across a composer with no training that managed to create a truly original work. More often than not, an untrained composers' compositions consist of a combination of several different theoretical approaches to composing that other composers have already worked out. A lack of knowledge to apply these approaches in the most elegant manner often results in lesser versions of a more established composer's work.

With formal study, a composer can learn how composers of the past created their works. After learning these techniques exist, the student may decide to dig deeper into these techniques to develop their musical works further. It's easy to believe that your music is original if you don't know what already exists in the world. Refusing to learn theory makes the path of composing more arduous than necessary.

Composers can start by finding the system or composer that reflects the music they want to be writing. Once the system is uncovered and digested, it's possible to branch out and write truly original music. It's not necessary to study every system under the sun, but it's very useful to seek out the composers and styles that can serve as practical tutors within a particular style. While this book focuses on classical-style concepts, there are many valid theories and musical styles available. Whether a composer is studying western or non-western music, learning the theories that exist for a particular style can accelerate the progression to truly original musical works.

Musical study helps composers progress from a beginner who scrutinizes every action to an expert who navigates the musical spheres using a combination of experience, intellect, and intuition. The tenets of music composition provide a foundation, but this must be nothing more than a starting point. After learning the principles that make the music of the past so effective, the composer must move forward and look toward the future. Clues for the music of the future are already embedded in the centuries of musical works at our disposal, but a composer must have the knowledge and experience necessary to uncover these gems of musical composition.

The Importance of Tradition

Composers who want to apply the concepts in this book in a practical way should start by composing in a traditional manner. This means the composer should learn to compose using standard music notation. Standard music notation may make it more difficult to compose initially, but the composer will develop increased proficiency and learn to notate even the most complex music with enough practice.

The tradition of writing music by hand offers a sound pedagogical approach that allows composers to connect with each individual note and think carefully about the musical composition. Writing by hand using pencil and staff paper requires the student to think about every pitch set to paper. Avoid using a notation program for simple melodies and two- to four-part works. When writing complex chamber and symphonic music, using a notation program can provide a significant time savings. However, these larger works can usually be reduced to one or two piano staves before approaching the notation program.

Electronic music is a valid means of composing music, but it tends to rely on chance and pre-existing materials to build a work in popular music. Creating electronic music of this nature accesses a different set of skills and manner of thinking when compared with notation-based composing. Building a composition from a collection of sounds and samplers usually results in the composer compromising to some extent. At some point, the musician must determine whether they want to be a *composer* who creates the materials needed for a new structure or an *arranger* who takes what is already available to create derivative music.

Both the composer and the arranger have valid viewpoints, but the composer can create virtually anything that can be notated or developed. The arranger is limited to what sample packages, loops, and pre-recorded material they have on hand.

A composer who can't notate musical ideas lacks a crucial mechanism for the editing and perfection of a musical work. Notation in itself is a system, but it's an open system that allows composers to make a substantial array of choices and relentlessly edit their works in great detail. Composers who study the concepts discussed in this book are working toward creating expansive and innovative musical works that function as a cohesive whole. After establishing a solid understanding of how to write traditional music, it's then possible to expand and use other methods. Some examples of novel (but not new) avenues for exploration include the possible implementation of microtones and non-standard notation systems to create musical works.

A solid understanding of the musical repertoire will go a long way toward the development of new musical structures and designs. Don't fall for the myth of the composer who is struck by a fit of inspiration that results in a great masterpiece. While this does happen to composers from time to time, the typical day for a composer is often a bit more mundane and consists of lots of editing and problem-solving. Intuition is an important part of composing a musical work that the composer can connect with on a deep level; however, inspiration can only come at a level the composer can comprehend. Inspiration that comes in a form beyond the composers' mental faculties is hard to realize in a concrete form such as notation. A composer who is inspired to write a new work can only notate as far as their technique allows. Trained composers have a higher ceiling to work with and are able to create more sophisticated musical works due to their technique.

The traditional approach to composing music relies on music notation and memory to manipulate ideas and create new sounds. Refusing to learn to notate musical ideas puts the composer at a disadvantage. Electronic music provides some truly incredible options for composing, but it's critical to understand how to notate and edit music through the visual representation that notation allows.

Becoming a master of the craft requires assimilation and working knowledge of many tools. Notation offers an effective tool for notating ideas and editing a composition in a concrete and intentional manner. The composer who understands how music developed and knows how to create their own materials using music notation is in a prime position to create something truly new and refreshing.

[this page intentionally left blank]

Patterns Are Everywhere

Humans are phenomenal at recognizing patterns. People can find patterns in any work of literature, art, music, and nature itself. Many artists feel a need to avoid patterns and create music intuitively, but these patterns often turn up anyway since humans are wired for pattern recognition and creation. Audiences respond to logical patterns, and it makes sense to locate the patterns in a musical work to take advantage of their power to create coherence. What may initially seem like a random spattering of notes on the page could turn into an intelligent, sophisticated, and accessible work if the composer takes the time to find and develop any existing patterns.

Bach once stated he could create a musical composition out of a random selection of notes. He proved his premise by creating a composition using only the letters of his name. In German, the letter h is a B-natural. Bach used the letters in his name (B-A-C-H) to compose a musical work. Composers can implement the same sort of inventive thinking. Look for the patterns in a musical work to develop a composition and create coherence for the audience.

Each motive, melody, phrase, and section introduce problems that need to be solved on an intellectual level. When pure intuition guides a composer, the result is almost always a work that is a mishmash of the techniques and styles assimilated from listening to other composers. A compilation of techniques may not provide enough substance for an audience to understand how a piece is developing. When techniques are employed in an intuitive way, and the audience is often left scratching their heads. A purely intuitive application of another composers' technique may result in an original and effective work, or it may result in a cacophony of sound that makes no musical sense.

Learn how to recognize the patterns in a musical work and extract the roadmap inherent within to create music that makes sense to the audience. If you're a composer, you should aim to play through a composition several times in your mind before setting a note to paper. Don't attempt to notate anything until you have memorized the work internally in your mind's ear. Once you notate the music, you can begin to edit the piece based on concepts introduced in this book.

The Overtone Series

When a single pitch sounds, there are also a series of less audible pitches that sound above the initial tone. These tones are known as overtones. The initial pitch, known as the fundamental, actually repeats several times in the overtone series at increasingly smaller intervals. Since the initial pitch is repeated the most often and gets support from the fainter overtones (think of this as tones *over* the *tones* of the fundamental), it's heard as the loudest pitch. The fundamental pitch serves as the foundation for all the overtones in the series.

Tones in the series can be references as partials or overtones. The difference between the two is subtle:

- A partial can be any note in the series, including the fundamental note.
- An overtone must be one of the notes that occurs above the fundamental.

If you wanted to identify the second note in the overtone series, you could refer to it as the first overtone or the second partial.

In modern notation, the notes of the overtone series have been tempered to fit Western music's concept of 12 equally spaced chromatic pitches. The notes listed in the image for the overtone series are only an approximate representation of the actual notes heard in the overtone series. The notes with accidentals written with parentheses in the series indicate notes that are either naturally sharp (high) or flat (low) compared to the natural overtones. When it came time to settle on the notes for the chromatic scale, musicians decided to use a 12-note scale and *temper* any notes that didn't fit. This resulted in an equal distance between each half-step in the chromatic scale. Thus, our tempered chromatic musical scale was formed.

If musicians used only the notes that occurred naturally in the overtone series, most of the notes would end up sounding just a little out of tune. In our modern system of notation, A♭ and G♯ are considered to be enharmonically related. An enharmonic set of pitches are represented by different notes on the staff that sound the same to the ear. In the past, the A♭ sounded slightly higher than the G♯. When the notes of our scale were tempered to create 12 equal pitches, these two notes merged to create a single pitch.

In the pure overtone series, some of our tempered notes match with the natural overtones more closely than others. In relation to the fundamental tone, the perfect unison, perfect fourth, perfect fifth, and perfect octave are so close to pitches in the overtones series that they don't have to be tempered. This is one reason why they are referred to as perfect intervals instead of major intervals. Tempering all of the notes in our 12-note system makes it possible to command massive orchestral forces with the entire ensemble playing in tune. Tempering the system also makes it much easier to memorize the sounds of intervals since a major or minor second will maintain the same distance between each pitch no matter what note you use as the starting point.

When listening to music of other cultures, pay attention to the melody and harmony. In many cases, you'll find that music that is not based on the tempered system tends to focus more on the melodic aspects of music than a tempered system does. This is why Western music tends to have large orchestral forces with several different instruments that play their own part. The tempered system tends to emphasize dense and complex harmonies while the overtone series in its purer form tends to emphasize melodic and rhythmic aspects. No system is perfect, and there are pros and cons to both systems.

The tempered system is not natural, and it is also not the only acceptable system for the creation of music. Composers must learn to recognize the different intervals and chords heard in music. Humans are not born with the knowledge that there are 12 pitches in music; it is knowledge we learn from our environment. People who are born with perfect pitch may very likely have an aptitude for identifying the many colors and hues in music in much the same way children can be taught to identify colors in the spectrum.

One thing to understand about music and the overtone series is that all of the pitches heard in music are just frequencies. In response to these frequencies, the eardrums vibrate, and through a rather complex process, pitches are heard as sounding high or low. Low pitches have slower vibrations and high pitches have faster vibrations.

Imagine a string on the violin. If the string is cut in half, the rate that the string vibrates will double when the violinist draws the bow across the string. This increases the pitch of the string by an octave. Further divisions of the string can also be made so that all of the pitches in the chromatic scale can be played.

Hearing the Overtones

Normally, it's difficult to hear the overtones that emanate from a single note. Luckily, the existence of the overtone series can be demonstrated with an experiment if you have an acoustic piano. This does not work on an electronic piano. I do have an example and deeper discussion of the overtone series on my YouTube channel:

(https://www.youtube.com/channel/UCUl4QRaP3JAsyBoCnhxTi6Q)

Located under The Musical Core Playlist Video 2.8.

1. Lightly hold down the notes C, E, and G on the piano. Press gently enough to avoid playing any of the notes. The goal is to rest the hammers inside the piano against the strings without striking hard enough to make any sound.

2. Strike a C an octave below the chord forcefully. Listen carefully. Notice that the notes that are held down will resonate and waver in and out.

3. Release the keys and quietly hold down the notes D, F, and A on the piano while striking the same C an octave below. These notes won't resonate as strongly because they are more remote overtones in the series and don't have the same connection to the fundamental (lowest pitch) in the C overtone series.

4. Release the keys again and hold down B♭. Now, hit C an octave below middle C. The B♭ should resonate slightly, but it might not be audible since the natural B♭ in the overtone series does not occur in our tempered musical system.

5. Experiment with other notes and you'll be able to develop a deeper understanding of how certain pitches resonate with underlying fundamental tones.

This effect occurs because the fundamental tone C has the overtones of C–E–G within the first two octaves. Since the notes C–E–G occur so early on in the series, they are strong overtones that can be heard clearly when their fundamental is struck.

The tempered musical system that grew out of the overtone series resolved the issue of unequal spacing of pitches. Without the tempered system, composers would have to deal with a more complicated system. In today's music, an interval of a minor third consists of three equally spaced half steps. The minor third will sound characteristically the same whether the starting pitch is a C, D, E, F, G, A, or B. In the past, this wasn't the case and it caused problems of intonation in performance when combined with other instruments.

To experience the overtone series in a musical work, look for a performance of a composition that uses a natural horn. Listening to a natural horn is a completely different musical experience from the tempered system. To our tempered ears, many of the notes will sound poorly tuned.

Schillinger System of Music Composition

"My system does not circumscribe the composer's freedom, but merely points out the methodological way to arrive at a decision. Any decision, which results in a harmonic relation, is fully acceptable. We are opposed only to vagueness and haphazard speculation."

~Schillinger

Joseph Moiseyevich Schillinger created a system that he believes makes it possible for anyone to compose effective music with intention. *The Schillinger System of Music Composition* offers an impressive tome of formulas and procedures, but the goal is not the procedures themselves. Instead, Schillinger wants composers to be intentional about composition. He believes there needs to be a relationship between harmonies, melodies, and rhythm for a piece to work effectively. The system is designed to provide composers with a four-year course in music composition, but as with any system, it is not without its limitations. *The Schillinger System of Music Composition* creates music that sounds harmonious, and it assumes the composer will compose in a mostly tonal style. It prescribes procedural concepts to create music, but this result may come at the expense of thinking about and solving the tough riddles inherent in the process of composing.

Schillinger's method informs the composer that when a musical event occurs, a series of possible paths may be followed. While his text proposes several options, the composer still has some great flexibility in making their own decisions. In this way, his theory makes it possible for other composers to create their own theories and put them into practice. This system may appeal to tonally bound composers who want a more analytical approach to composing music. As a technique, it can result in a surprising array of music, but the system may also lock a composer into a single genre since the system supports the creation of a set of rules and practices that are determined ahead of time.

Schillinger doesn't take into full account the manner in which all of the elements in a musical work effect the coherence and development of a composition. The Schillinger System assumes that there are only a few correct ways to compose music, and most of the correct methods are based very heavily in the tonality of the nineteenth and early twentieth century, even if the text does claim to allow a composer to write in any style.

An explanation of how the Schillinger system works is beyond the scope of this text, but composers should know the system was created in the 1930s when it was believed that truth was more absolute, and basic principles existed in the sciences as well as art. Music was viewed as a natural phenomenon to be conquered with underlying formulas and principles waiting to be revealed. This gives the Schillinger system a very demanding point of view. It uses a series of mathematical equations and principles to explain music composition, and it provides composers with procedures and guidelines to follow during the creative process.

With the goal of providing composers with a system designed to create music quickly, the system necessarily left out many of the nuanced principles of composition that master composers spent their lives trying to comprehend. However, the system is not without its merits. The Schillinger System was *partially* used to compose George Gershwin's *Porgy and Bess* and Glenn Miller's *Moonlight Serenade*. These are classic works that are still performed widely today. *The Addams Family* and *Green Acres* soundtracks were also created with elements *inspired* from the system. Pay special attention to the words *partially* and *inspired*. In most of these cases, the composer added unique stylistic points to make the technique their own. However, no musical work can truly be unique if it uses outside techniques to solve problems at the expense of searching for the answers within the unique configuration of notes in the work itself.

Composers who study the Schillinger system with the intent of gathering additional tools will benefit from the four-year course. The system strips some musicality from the process of composing and replaces it with a system designed to compose music that functions in a time-tested manner. Talented composers will be able to use the system to create substantial works, but as with any system, the composer must learn to be creative within its confines.

Composers who are interested in writing film music should seek out and study the *Schillinger System of Music Composition*. However, it's important for composers to maintain perspective and realize that learning the system does not mean the composer will reach the summit of all that may be learned about music composition. Learning the craft of music composition is something that takes both intuition and the assimilation of several ideas, and no one method is going to work universally well for all composers.

If you use the Schillinger method, just remember that you are learning about the craft of music composition. While Schillinger aims to press this point and make it clear, the distinction can often get lost once proficiency in the system is attained. Use the system as a guide to check your compositions, but avoid using the Schillinger system as a substitute for the creation of art. *This principle applies to any system; not just Schillinger's.*

Twelve-Tone System of Music Composition

"Composition with twelve tones has no other aim than comprehensibility."

~ Arnold Schoenberg

The *Twelve-Tone System of Music Composition* is the result of the work of Arnold Schoenberg. At its most basic level, 12-tone is a system that is designed to obscure the concept of tonality. Depending on how for you take it, the system can be used freely in an atonal style or in a more formulaic and intentional way where all 12 chromatic pitches are played in succession before returning to the initial pitch. This results in a musical work where the listener is unable to identify a single pitch that the melody revolves around. In most music, the first and last notes tend to be the same pitch.

Schoenberg is most often credited with the creation of 12-tone music. Despite claims from other composers who believed they created the system first, nobody else developed the concept of atonality to the level of Schoenberg's system. Regardless of the disputes, history recognizes Schoenberg as the originator of the system, and he certainly did more than any other composer to outline the system's techniques and procedures.

Twelve-tone music is a subset of atonal music, and one of the goals of 12-tone is to avoid placing an emphasis on a tonal center. This system possesses passion for following a set of directives, but that is only the result of how composers and musicians have responded to the system. These rules are not necessarily an indication of how the system was intended to be used, and it's not how Schoenberg used the system.

Schoenberg didn't create the system to help other composers write music. According to Schoenberg, he simply analyzed his own music and uncovered these principles. He was an advocate of composing music entirely in your mind and not plucking out notes on an instrument. In fact, in some circles, there used to be a stigma associated with composers who would rely on a piano to compose music. In effect, Schoenberg felt that gaining a knowledge of the system he developed to compose his own works would help him take the system further and support his original compositions. He could also teach the principles of his music and aide younger composers in understanding the system. It's important to note that Schoenberg did not create the system so other composers could copy and mass manufacture his compositions.

Schoenberg reasoned that it was time to open the world's ears to a new type of music that was unlike any music previously composed. He envisioned that both composers and audiences would be inspired by "tone-color melodies," which he referred to as *Klangfarbenmelodie*. He had a highly developed ear, and he could pick out the different tones and interval combinations that were used in complex chords. This made it easier for him to follow *Klangfarbonmelodie* in a composition. While some may say this alienated the listener, Schoenberg was very adamant about his believe that "if it is art, it is not for all." Though, you don't have to take such a strict point of view to appreciate or write music. Schoenberg can be rather intense in his views, and intensity can often blind a person to alternatives. It should also be noted that Schoenberg's last word was reportedly *Harmony*, which is a component that many people believe is missing in his music. If that's not eerie enough, he also seems to have predicted the day he would die.

In a 12-tone work, most people don't hear the melodies because the sequence of 12 tones is repeated so quickly and obscurely that it's very difficult to recognize the sequences, transmutations, and permutations in his melodies. One solution to reduce the obscurity of the sequence was to simplify the melody and create coherence by using rhythm as a unifying force.

Research suggests listeners are inclined to recognize the rhythm in a piece ahead of pitch sequences, so it's logical for rhythm to play a critical role with abstract melodies. Despite the efforts to make the system's music accessible to listeners, atonality and its branches resulted in the audience having difficulty following the complex pitch patterns. For many people, the music ended up sounding like a wash of sound with many people flatly calling it out as noise.

Schoenberg believed that the 12-tone system was the next most logical step towards a more honest system of musical composition. Acoustic instruments used in orchestras and ensembles are limited in their ability to play the tones of the chromatic system. Schoenberg reasoned that to break away from tonality, he would first need to open up the listener's ear to stop labeling consonant textures as good and dissonant musical textures as bad. He preferred to think of consonance and dissonance as different colorings that the ear could become accustomed to appreciating. Rather than pleasing and non-pleasing sounds, Schoenberg wanted a world that recognized all sounds as valid and on a scale that ranged from consonant to dissonant.

Schoenberg also wrote a standard theory textbook entitled, *The Theory of Harmony*. In this text, he delves into the role of the overtone series, which is a concept that helps to explain the logic behind our major and minor scales. His theory of harmony goes through all of the standard chord construction procedures one might expect from a theory text, but there is no inclusion of form and analysis. He ends with a discussion of more advanced techniques, including a discussion of ninth chords, modern scales, and chords constructed in fourths. Schoenberg's *Theory of Harmony* is dynamic and engaging, and it's an interesting read to learn more about the nature of music and the concept of aesthetics.

Blocking the Evolution of Art

Any system used by a composer to compose a new work runs the risk of turning into a collection of techniques that takes the burden of solving complex compositional problems off the composer. Systems are useful in that they grant composers access to techniques that can be used to enhance musical compositions. But a composer must also be well-versed in how the elements of music composition function in a larger work to create music that breaks the rules when a better opportunity presents itself.

When composers learn a system, they are only learning how to compose music using a very specific set of rules. In contrast, an understanding of *the aesthetics of music* builds an arsenal of tools that work together to bring to life music based on sound principles, flexible techniques, and purposeful attention to all the elements of the work.

Tonal music is also a system that could have been referenced, and there are several techniques that come out of that system. In this vein, the Schillinger system is akin to the tonal system of music composition since it can be used to create a variety of styles and musical works, albeit within the limitations of an essentially tonal work. Schoenberg's 12-tone music is limited in how it may be applied, but it's also a system that he devised on his own to explain the logic of his musical works.

The 12-tone and Schillinger system are highlighted to illustrate the limitations inherent with learning music theory and other systems for composing music. Any system of theory could have been used, including Schenkerian analysis, Riemannian theory, set theory, or a number of other possibilities to make the same point. While the two systems addressed are designed to create logical musical works, the founders have dramatically different motivations for creating each system;

- Schillinger developed a system that emphasizes tonality.
- Schoenberg developed a system that breaks tonality.

Based on these contrasting points of view, these two systems provide a case for two contrasting styles of music composition. In the case of Schillinger's system, students learned how to compose music that was primarily scientific in its implementation and can be applied in a wide range of musical styles. Schoenberg's system is more narrowly defined, and it was intended to showcase the aspects of his own music works.

The Schillinger system was designed to solve the limitations of music theory and provide a system that could be used to create effective music. The Schillinger system provides the possibility for a host of different outcomes that may result in radically different compositions, but the end result is that composers may become dependent on theories and rules to ensure their musical works conform to the system.

Schoenberg's 12-tone is also a system. The intention was to create a diverse system that would emancipate composers from predominantly consonant works. Ultimately, he desired to break the world out of the dependence on tonality. He also stated that the system was one that he naturally gravitated toward, and it was not contrived simply to create something different.

In many ways, Schoenberg and Schillinger worked toward similar goals. Both composers thought their system could eventually offer a way forward from tonality.

Ultimately, Schoenberg did not believe in the philosophy of using systems or laws to compose music. In the work, *Schoenberg: His Life, World, and Work* by Hans Heinz Stuckenschmidt, Schoenberg is famously quoted as saying, "My works are 12-tone *compositions*, not *12-tone* compositions." In the text *Immanence and Transcendence*, Schoenberg also criticized how his music was played stating, "My music is not modern, it is merely badly played." The realization that Schoenberg himself didn't approve of how his music was performed illustrates the assertion that, at heart, the composer had one foot firmly planted in romanticism with the other stretching toward the twentieth century.

One aim of Schoenberg's music was to compose works that matched his worldview. He often remarked on how he would compose his works on walks and not think about the theory until the final stages of the editing process. (Another composer who walks). The Schillinger system works in an opposing manner, which is to create music based almost entirely on a system.

What readers can learn from the comparison of these systems is that the creation of a system to detail the theory behind a particular composer's music stands in stark contrast to the way these systems of theory are often used in practice. Often, theory is used to gauge the effectiveness of a work and help a composer to create music in an existing style.

Schoenberg created a system to explain his music, and you should attempt to do the same. Though, it's important to avoid getting bogged down in the details. Don't make the mistake of thinking your system can never evolve and develop.

Schoenberg's system is intended to change the perception that dissonance was to be avoided, or sneakily moved past, as a means of pushing a composition towards a consonant resolution. During his time, consonance was often considered to be desirable and beautiful while dissonance was considered ugly. By composing with 12 tones and following the guidelines outlined in the system, Schoenberg had the lofty goal of reducing the dependence on tonality. The system served to break audiences and musicians out of tonality and come to terms with a wider definition and conception of music. Since tonality had a large strangle-hold on music, Schoenberg created a system that made it possible to open our ears to a completely new style of music, and he broke the dam preventing new compositional ideas from springing forth.

For those who are still on the fence about Schoenberg and his relationship to his 12-tone system, one very telling quote from his *Theory of Harmony* text should convert some detractors. Schoenberg emphatically states throughout the text that systems are only useful as methods to better understand and learn about music that has already been composed. This is evidenced clearly and without hesitation when Schoenberg makes clear his disdain for systems that place theory above art:

"To hell with all these theories, if they always only serve to block the evolution of art and if their positive achievement consists in nothing more than helping those who will compose badly to learn it quickly . . . The laws of art consist mainly of exceptions."

Schillinger created a system that is flexible, but in many ways is also absolute since he creates rules for composers to create music. It proposes laws and encourages composers to develop a scientific relationship to music. What is most interesting about Schillinger's method is that it is a system that is designed to teach composition. Most theories don't claim to teach students how to be composers; rather, they teach musicians about commonalities in music and how to recognize these components in a musical work.

The Schillinger System of Music Composition offers a useful system that composers can use to create works, but the system can also serve the goal of propping up the composer until better technique allows for the creation of works unfettered by convention. Since the intent of the system was to make many decisions for the composer, it ends up acting as a negative influence on the evolution of art. Schoenberg's system was designed to break the bonds of the permissible and non-permissible in music, and so it serves the lofty goal of helping composers to break free of a long tradition that aims to dictate what can be written by a composer.

If a system becomes a crutch the composer relies on to create new works, then the system is serving "only to block the evolution of art." It essentially boils down to whether the composer wants to use a system as means to a loftier end to create something new or use it as the means itself and mimic composers of the past.

Toward a New Tonality

Both Schoenberg and Schillinger created systems. Schoenberg's system concentrates on pantonality while Schillinger's focuses on tonality. These systems, and others, set the stage for future developments in music. However, to fully appreciate how tonality and atonality set the stage for a new tonality, it's necessary to go back to the overtone series.

The overtone series offers a clue to one possible future in music. Ultimately, Schoenberg work went a long way toward abolishing the strictures of tonality and leading the world to a more fluid concept of consonance and dissonance, where all levels of dissonance are accepted. Rather than stating consonance is good and dissonance is bad, he argued that each interval or chord has its own character that should be appreciated.

Our modern chromatic scale could have been divided into any number of smaller divisions, but the system was designed with 12 equally spaced half steps to maintain an equal distance between each chromatic note. A pure and natural octave with evenly spaced pitches that matched the overtone series would require over 3,000 notes in the octave. Since that's not realistic, the most viable option that mostly works on a mathematical level is the 12-note scale. Hence, the western system of 12 equally spaced notes was born, and over the centuries composers developed effective ways for manipulating those notes to create musical works.

Schoenberg was aware of the overtone series and recognized the problems inherent in the tempered system of music. While he wanted a more natural scale, he decided it was important to work with what was available. He even created a system of notation that used microtones, which are the tones that fall in between the half steps of a chromatic scale. String instruments are capable of performing microtones without adjusting the instrument. Microtones are more difficult to play than standard notes, but modern string players can and do play these pitches when they are indicated in the score. Other instruments require a more advanced technique to play microtones, and it may even be impossible on some instruments.

Thanks to the research completed by Dr. Robert Neumann, Schoenberg knew that more notes were needed in the chromatic scale to create a scale that more naturally conformed with the pure, unmodified overtone series. As mentioned previously, to have a completely natural scale that was perfectly in line with the overtones in nature, the scale would need to include several thousand notes within a single octave. As a compromise, Dr. Neumann proposed a 53-note scale, but it would still be a nightmare to perform a piece with 53 notes per octave. Take a moment to imagine what the piano would have to look like to include 53 notes per octave. A standard piano has a range of eight octaves plus a minor third, which results in 88 keys. A piano with 53 notes per octave would need more than 420 keys!

Schoenberg knew that a full complement of orchestral instruments required to perform microtones on a large scale wouldn't exist in his lifetime. Rather than spending all his time writing music that couldn't be performed, Schoenberg did the next best thing and created the *12-Tone System of Music Composition* to start the process of breaking away from the limitations of an imperfect scale. The goal of his method was partially to spur the advancement of music composition.

Schoenberg felt he could accomplish his goal of enhanced musical expression through the use of more natural scales only when the instruments became capable of performing additional tones. While the instruments to play 53 notes in a single scale still aren't available, electronic music does offer one possible route toward the realization of his goals. Still, he hoped that one day we would have more natural tones to work with, which is why he also played around with systems of notation to notate microtones in anticipation of the day when the chromatic scale was expanded.

People often overlook the fact that Schoenberg bridged the divide between the romantic and modern periods of music. He was a composer with one foot planted in the romantic era and another in the modern era. One can imagine Schoenberg thinking up the creation of new works in the distant future. He probably envisioned instruments capable of creating sounds from nature with motives that mimic natural phenomenon.

In Schoenberg's ideal system, the sound of rain falling and thunderous overtures that harnessed the power of complex *tone-color melodies* to vibrant effect would be the norm. Musicians tend to focus on the highly complex musical lines in his compositions as proof that he was overly academic and that his music should be played academically as well. Many musicians fail to realize that with Schoenberg, the music needs to be interpreted in an embellished and impassioned romantic style.

A less than ideal performance is a problem for all new composers, and it's not the performers fault. Performers have played Beethoven for nearly two centuries, and they know how to interpret his music. With new music, it's difficult to play the music effortlessly because there just isn't enough time to learn a piece. It takes years before a performer can truly play a work effortlessly. Until the work is embedded in the memory of the performer so deeply that it can be played fluently, it's very difficult to perform a work in a truly inspired manner.

Schoenberg's system was largely an attempt to secure the German musical tradition for the foreseeable future and push composers, and their audiences, to accept dissonances in music more readily. At its core, the system offers a method to create music that has no tonal center and relies only on the relationship between pitch and rhythm for "melodic" development. In a broader sense, the system provided the catalyst that the world needed to begin seriously exploring the dissonances in music and how they could be used to create new musical works.

Many composers who didn't understand the essence and purpose of the system relied on it to create music that lacked emotional depth and originality. The system unintentionally turned traditional compositional problems into mathematical ones in a manner similar to the *Schillinger System of Music Composition*. Alban Berg and other composers of the time, understood the spirit of the system and used it to create masterful works adhering to the rules when appropriate and abandoning them when a better option or intuition reared its head.

The goal of any musical system shouldn't be to compose music, but to provide a tested and proven way forward when lacking alternative options. It should also serve to show a composer what already exists and to help the musician identify what is unique to each composer. If a composer does something that doesn't fit with the guidelines of music theory, it is something the musician should pay attention to and consider in greater depth.

It is not the common language that music theory uncovers that makes a work great, but the inconsistencies in a particular musical work where a composer defies convention and creates something new.

For many composers who wrote in the 12-tone style, it was no longer a question of whether the chord progression had any relevance to the melody. Instead, it became a quest to employ the different forms of the 12-tone row in the cleverest way possible.

Many systems cut the *heart* out of the compositional process in favor of using only the *head*. The 12-tone and Schillinger systems make it possible for anybody to compose music using a structure, but structures can only take a composer to the heights of what has already been accomplished.

Ultimately, using a system will result in music that fails to treat each composition as a work of art that has its own needs. The great artist understands that the medium dictates the art, and the artist is a conduit for the medium to realize its potential. Understand the natural tendencies inherent in the elements of a musical work, and it's possible to create a composition that tells an exceptional musical story.

My personal belief is that we don't need to create 53 note scales or change any of the instruments we currently have available. I also am not convinced that 12-tone music was the next logical step from tonality. I believe that the next stage is to return to the overtone series. The structure of tonality relies largely on the dominant-tonic chord relationships that are based on the overtone series. However, I feel the strongest pull to the tonic is not the dominant, but another chord altogether. I'm also being intentionally vague about this *other chord* since I'm still working out the details myself.

Whether I'm right or wrong is less important than the fact that I can write fluidly in my system, and it stems from the result of years of study and knowledge of music theory and counterpoint. To move toward a new tonality, all composers should learn the tenets of music and dive deep into their own musical patterns to uncover the secret logic of their unconscious mind. The system I am going to propose in later chapters is flexible, without dogma, and easy to apply to most styles of composition. Within the system, you can begin to insert your own theories and beliefs about how music works.

The State of Music

"Prince, what you are, you are by accident of birth; what I am, I am through my own efforts. There have been thousands of princes and will be thousands more; there is only one Beethoven!"

~ Beethoven to Prince Lichnowsky

While there is some historical debate as to whether Beethoven actually said this to his benefactor, Prince Lichnowsky, it raises a crucial point about the act of composition. Any individual who composes music leaves a legacy in their wake. A musical work can live on long after the composer, and this makes it possible to create music that serves as a memory of a composer's existence.

Figure 1: A 1913 cartoon in Die Zeit mocking a Schoenberg concert.

Thanks to composers like Schoenberg, there is now massive freedom to compose music in any style and use any technique available to accomplish musical goals. With so many different genres of music, there isn't one style that stands out as the predominant contemporary style. However, when it comes to the traditional methods of connecting motives and developing a composition, much of the 20th century European tradition of concert music developed in a way that many people feel alienated musicians and audiences alike.

Schoenberg and his compatriots were collectively known as the Second Viennese School. Along with his pupils Berg and Webern, this group was known for their atonality in the early 20th century. The group initially composed music that aimed to expand tonality, and then later it grew into atonality, and eventually 12-tone.

The Second Viennese School with Schoenberg, Berg, and Webern at the helm had critics proclaiming that their inferior music was causing chaos and defying the fundamental principles of music. While their music is now more widely accepted today, the music of the Second Viennese School of composers indicates that the world is still not yet ready to appreciate this highly dense and complex music. Even though there is a resistance to this type of music, many musicians who gain familiarity with the music develop a love for these compositions.

Atonal music can be dense, complex, and hard to follow. The music isn't for everyone, but the complex nature of the music is one of the qualities that makes the music worth trying to appreciate. Even for those who never develop a love for this music, the exposure to new kinds of music can help open the mind and ear to new sonic possibilities.

The Second Viennese School opened up our minds to what was possible in music. Because of the efforts of these composers, our ear for dissonance has been expanded to accommodate a more encompassing definition of what is acceptable in music. That kind of freedom is priceless. The early 20th century made dissonance acceptable, and composers now have a much wider selection of tools at their disposal.

Composers who write orchestral and chamber music are in a state of experimentation right now. In many ways, composers are going through a new Baroque period in music.

The Baroque period experienced great progress in the development of tonality, which came as the result of extensive experimentation. The time periods that followed served to refine and establish tonality with Mozart perfecting the style. Beethoven pushed music forward and acted as a bottleneck – composers either wrote like Beethoven or withered in obscurity. Later, composers like Gustav Mahler and Wagner took tonality to the breaking point. When Schoenberg came along, the composers of his time effectively broke tonality and opened the floodgates to an unprecedented variety of music.

Many opera companies and orchestras tend to only feature works from classical and romantic period composers, even though new works are steadily created. However, finding a venue for performance has proven difficult for many composers. Rather than taking this as an insinuation that modern music is not welcome, composers need to take it upon themselves to get their music in front of the public to encourage audiences to gain familiarity with their works.

Some may argue that modern music has not had a substantial audience in quite some time, but this should not deter young composers from attempting to break into the music scene. Composers who feel a calling to write music are going to compose regardless of the current musical environment. The biggest obstacle for a composer is getting new music performed by risk-averse orchestras and attracting new audiences to the concert hall.

Steven Stucky asked a poignant question to connections in his social network before his untimely passing, and I was lucky enough to be a part of that exchange. He noted how people kept stating that classical music was obsolete. The conversation took off from there, and many insightful observations were made by several musicians and composers. The general consensus was that concert music will not die as long as there are composers and performers willing to keep it alive.

Of course, just because music is being kept propped up by life support in some arenas, it also doesn't necessarily mean that classical music is thriving. Still, composers are compelled to create for inexplicable reasons, and it's something that they are going to continue to engage in and schedule time for in their lives. Any composer who aims to write music should take on the mindset that if something is worth doing, it's important enough to take the time to do it right. For a composer, this means taking the time to learn the principles that make music work.

With no guarantee that any living composer will enter the history books, composers simply have to write music that aligns with their personal preferences and beliefs. Richard Strauss was considered a major composer in his time. Many music historians now view his works as less influential when compared to Gustav Mahler. This is interesting because Mahler was a lesser known composer during his life, and most of his acclaim during his life was granted for his conducting abilities. The music of Strauss tends to be difficult to analyze while Mahler's music was too dissonant for the audiences of his time.

The fame Strauss received during his lifetime was enough to secure him a spot in the history books. While it took more time for Mahler's music to gain acceptance, the quality of his music eventually set the standard for the next generation. Mahler was ahead of his time, which made it difficult for people to appreciate where his musical vision was leading. Like Mozart, he was not truly famous until after his death.

Only time determines the music that survives the gauntlet of public opinion. The issue of what music will be deemed representative of our time period is not a new problem. This problem has been with music for as long as composers have been writing. A composer can only worry about writing great music and getting it performed. Let the question of whether it will be remembered lay on the shoulders of future generations. Composers who have gained popularity during their life have historically had no guarantee of success with future generations.

Composers influence each other in various ways. Mahler was an influence on Wagner, Mozart influenced Beethoven and Haydn influenced all of the classical composers either through direct instruction or notoriety. The chromatics of Wagner's

68

music still finds appeal among the concertgoers of today. While all of this is interesting, it may be a waste of time for a composer to worry about such things. Any composer with a desire to be included in the ranks of the finest composers should aim to learn as much about the history of music as possible and compose diligently. In this way, it will become possible to recognize trends and potentially see where the future of music is headed. And if the future is not headed in a direction that agrees with the composer, they always have the option of spending their life trying to change the direction.

Young composers should learn the craft thoroughly and not worry too much about the current state of music. Don't attempt to write music to fit the current trends. Write the music that calls to you, and edit it relentlessly using your knowledge of the mechanics of music. Write consistently every day and let the chips fall where they may. If there isn't a market for your music, put in the work to create one. Many composers have created their own ensembles with colleagues and friends to get their music recognized and in front of the public. Get performances and stay active, and eventually, people may begin to listen to what you have to say in your music.

The question you should ask yourself is whether you can afford to ignore centuries of musical development in favor of gimmicks and performance art.

Below are just a few of the questions that might crop up as you begin to study theory through the centuries and come to your own conclusions about what music theory means to you.

- Is it wise to ignore the lessons of the masters of the past?
- Is walking through a park and listening to the sounds of nature *music* or an *experience*, and should you care to define the difference?
- How can you use the process of analyzing a piece using standard techniques and apply it to your own compositions?

A Final Note About Systems of Music

Systems don't create art; people create art.

It's certainly scarier and harder to put a composition out into the world that is based on personal insights, observations, and training. However, the reward is the creation of unique and authentic music. Composers who take the time to understand what exists end up creating original works and not music that is based on another composer's system of musical composition.

The study of music composition should follow an integrated approach as the composition student develops fundamental skills. A composer's education should integrate subjects that traditionally are taught separately such as theory, orchestration, instrumentation, counterpoint, and form. However, devising such a system is also a monumental task. Schoenberg attempted to do this during his lifetime, but he was never able to complete his work. Luckily, Schoenberg laid the groundwork for composers to pursue an in-depth training program for a complete theory of music composition. The groundwork exists in many of his lesser-known works and writings, but it requires some reading between the lines to benefit from his incomplete texts. Schoenberg's ultimate goal was a text that taught all of the elements of music composition in a linear and practical manner, but this goal remained unrealized.

In fact, no composer or theorist has yet created a single unified theory that teaches the many disparate disciplines in an organized and thoughtful manner. Application to real-world situations is what is missing in most theory, counterpoint, and form texts. *The Elements of Music Composition* helps composers to begin that journey, but it can never truly complete the journey because composing is ultimately an individual expression.

Systems are inherently sluggish, but they serve a worthy purpose. A composer may put in great efforts to understand and learn a system, but once the system is mastered, the obligation to think critically about a musical work can lose priority.

Instead of focusing on the art, the composer may focus too much on whether the composition adheres to the guidelines established by the system.

Many composers enjoy the sense of security that a system offers since it removes much of the risk associated with composing something that might fail. After all, a composer who follows the system correctly can place the blame for any failure of the work on an unsophisticated audience or the system that was employed in the creation of the work.

Composers can easily rationalize how it was the system that was at fault, and this can act as a shield that deflects any blame for a failed work. When a system is not used, the poor reception of a musical work is completely at the feet of the composer. The writer can then go through the piece, find any weaknesses and improve on the next composition. When an established method is used, it's tempting to blame the system and put in more hours of studying to uncover the reason a newly minted composition was not received with universal acclaim. In most cases, *it's not the system that failed*, but the fact that the audience simply didn't connect with the message the composer tried to convey. Systems produce effective but disingenuous music that isn't authentic, and even the most casual listener can often sense a lesser copy of another composers' genius.

Despite the issues, systems do have benefits. Practically speaking, systems can help composers secure a commercial music job since an established method enables the ability to write quickly on a tight deadline. Getting a job is certainly a good reason to want to learn to use any method of composition. Companies and the movie industry love composers who use systems because they deliver reliable, fast, and consistent results. A filmmaker who chooses a composer who uses a system often respects the composer because all of the composer's music tends to have a similar level of quality.

A composer who strives to get away from systems to write original works takes on more risk since the composition might not work out exactly as intended and often takes more time to complete. Without a system, each new work is a challenge to the composer.

If you have a valid reason to use and absorb a system, then I suggest you find one that helps you compose the music you want to write more quickly. Commercial composers need a system to keep deadlines and produce on a schedule. Even if you make your living composing music that is not truly original, spend some time composing for yourself and the future of music as well.

Systems won't solve every problem, and a certain degree of skill is required to learn and apply them in an effective way. No matter how a composer approaches the creation of a new work, writing music is difficult and time-consuming. The employment of a system doesn't prevent the development of an original voice and style; however, for the composer who wants to create a musical work that truly stands out, the only way forward involves moving beyond the system to create new music that promotes a personal structural truth while still acknowledging the accomplishments of the past.

Composing with hard and fast rules can result in compositions that are lacking in creativity and awareness since it's easy to let the rules take over and dictate how a composition unfolds. While focusing on the rules and processes, composers can easily lose track of the bigger picture. The composer may blindly focus on how well the sequences and permutations fit within the parameters of the current procedure. Systems put composers at risk of halting intelligent and creative thought. Perhaps most importantly, strict adherence to rules can get in the way of a composer pondering the nature of the musical motives in the work and uncovering how the motives yearn to be molded, developed, and metamorphosed throughout the composition.

While it's critical to work out a method of composition that works for you, it's even more important to develop your ability to imagine and realize musical works. No matter what method is used, composers still need an ear that works, a good sense for melody, and the ability to imagine a piece in its entirety before committing a single note to paper. The details can be worked out once the composer starts notating, but the general ability to hear a piece unfold in the mind is critical for any composer.

Composers must develop their musicianship skills through a combination of ear training, listening to music, and practicing composing a musical work entirely in the mind. This may mean the composer starts by composing simple phrases, then adding a bass line, and expanding the work incrementally to develop and improve their musical memory. Ultimately, a system provides the foundation that a composer needs to establish their craft, but the composer can't venture out on their own until the training wheels are incinerated in the fires of progress.

The most damaging aspect of a system is the potential that a composer may use the rules and guidelines to provide hackneyed solutions to problems. Learning the difference between a solution that works and a solution that elevates a work is essential to writing an effective work. Solutions must be addressed on an individual basis where the answer to the problem arrives from within the composition itself. When compositional problems are solved using the materials and techniques already inherent within a composition, a musical work can flourish, grow, and develop on its own merits. While a system is virtually guaranteed to provide a solution that works, it abandons the possibility of finding other options that might take the musical work into new territory. Humans naturally want to create. Nothing stifles creativity more than an influx of the banal and ordinary.

Methods of composition don't usually address major problems such as why the orchestration causes the melody to sound muddy or lifeless. Even if the theory works out, the composer may be missing some crucial practical knowledge to help avoid problems while orchestrating a work. If all acts of composition could be relegated to a set of rules, then there would be no art in music. Too often, theories focus on one aspect of a musical work, such as the harmony, the motives, or the form. Ignoring the elements of music composition in favor of broader aspects of composing gives an unfaithful interpretation of the theory of composition.

Despite the problems with systems, mastering the various systems that do exist can play a crucial role in learning to compose music. When systems are used to promote the creation of new works, they end up serving a vital and useful process in the art of composing. The process of learning a system keeps the mind sharp and results in the development of composition technique. However, composers must strive to develop along a path that doesn't resort to formulas and processes as a substitute for original thought and introspection.

In the end, composers must trust their intuition and skill to create the music that resonates with them, systems are only the transport that serves to get the composer between the stages of creative ability and understanding.

PART III: COMPONENTS
ELEMENTS, CORNERSTONES, AND MOTIVES

Elements and Cornerstones serve as the basis for composing music. Composers should be aware of the ways that the various musical parts can combine to create motives and cornerstones in artistic work.

It's always seemed to me that instruments, in a certain sense, offer one materials for composition just by having, as they always do, built-in "character-structures," so to speak, which can be suggestive of musical possibilities both on the level of sonority and on that of actual musical behavior.

~ Elliot Carter

It's the music that has to be organized, not simply the notes. Because very often people assume that if you can find some kind of organization there, whether it is has any relation to what you actually hear or experience in hearing, or should think of in hearing, that then you're disposed of the problem...It has to be organized in terms of the musical ideas.

~ Henry Cowell

Elements, cornerstones, and motives are nearly inextricably intertwined, which makes it difficult to separate these concepts without referring to all components simultaneously. This part aims to deal with each concept individually, but it may be necessary to read through the elements, cornerstones, and motives sections several times before understanding these concepts.

As a teaching tool, you will also notice concepts are often repeated with different phrasing to help explain the idea of organic music in a linear fashion and provide more than one example of each integration. We begin with a discussion of functional versus non-functional elements and harmonies; but, understand that elements, cornerstones, and motives are usually related to each other in the context of this book.

While a discussion of these concepts is provided, readers without basic musicianship skills may find this part very dense and difficult to comprehend.

The goal in this section is not to explain concepts of pitch, elements, rhythm, dynamics, motives, and form, but to show how these components can be used to create cohesion in a musical work.

Components of Music

"All that is not perfect down to the smallest detail is doomed to perish."

~ Gustav Mahler

To organize some basic concepts, aspects of music have been compartmentalized into components referred to as elements, motives, and cornerstones. Without a solid understanding of the differences inherent within elements, motives, and cornerstones, it will be difficult to proceed through the remainder of the text and discuss organic music. In the following pages, these terms are defined and related to the subject matter in this text.

Elements Overview

Elements define music at the micro-level and can be used to construct motives and cornerstones.

Elements are the smallest components of a composition. They must be combined with a motive or cornerstone to function as part of a musical work and to give the piece coherence. With a definition this broad, an element can take many forms. In some cases, an element may serve the function of motive. In others, it won't be able to stand on its own. For example, a dynamic by itself is an element since dynamics can't create sound without a rhythm or melody to play the dynamic. A dynamic could be used in a motivic way if it is used in a way that brings attention to a particular melodic-motivic section.

Dynamics, articulations, tempos, rhythm, pitch, and even instrument timbre can all function as elements. These are not the only elements that can occur in a composition. With some creativity, other devices may also serve an elemental purpose, including measures, time signatures, breath marks, articulations, and fermatas.

Elements can serve a functional role, in which they work to fulfill some harmonic, melodic, or formal goal. Elements can also serve a non-functional role that is purely decorative in a composition. For elements to be memorable, you need at least two or more different elements to combine. For example, rhythm and pitch are two commonly combined elements. Almost all elements contain the element of either pitch or rhythm since it is difficult to create music without these two elements.

Motives Overview

Motives serve as a bridge or carrier between elements and cornerstones.

Motives are often made up of several elements since they require more than one element to be recognizable. Motives are a component that exists somewhere between an element and cornerstone.

While a motive isn't quite large enough to meet the general definition of a cornerstone, it does serve as a container or transport for the other elements. It's possible to reduce a motive to the point where it functions more like an element than a cornerstone. The versatility of a motive showcases its importance in your music; it works as a bridge between elements and cornerstones. Motives are extremely versatile and can be manipulated in many different ways.

Cornerstones Overview

Cornerstones define a piece at the macro-level.

Cornerstones are more significant components that contain at least two elements. Harmony, phrases, counterpoint, orchestration, and form are examples of cornerstones. These are subjects that are discussed in this text, but each of these subjects requires their own separate textbook and discipline.

Think of cornerstones as the container for musical elements. You can pour elements into a container to give a composition shape, and further define your musical work.

Cornerstones most often serve a functional role. Compositions that use cornerstones in a non-functional way may sound amateurish, vague, or confusing to the listener.

Functional vs. Non-Functional

It's important to remember that motives and cornerstones should play a functional role in your music.

- A functional role is one that is essential to the development of your piece.
- A non-functional component serves as decoration.

In most compositions, elements are the only components that may serve a non-functional role. As you gain proficiency, you can begin to think about ways to make a cornerstone or motive non-functional, but this should be undertaken with extreme care so that your composition doesn't feel like it's meandering or aimlessly wandering.

Now that we have established that only elements typically serve a non-functional role, let's go a bit deeper into the meaning of functional and non-functional roles:

Functional: A functional role plays a part in the development of your composition. Functional dynamic markings should serve to propel the piece toward a particular goal. The goal could be a cadence, the development of a motive, or some other objective.

Non-functional: A non-functional role typically provides ornamentation that adds shape to a melodic line, but it doesn't have characteristics that are unique enough to stand on their own as recognizable elements. When elements don't add to the coherence or design of the piece, then they are purely non-functional.

It's possible to think of functional and non-functional roles in the same way that functional and non-functional harmonies exist in common-practice music. Traditionally, functional and non-functional roles are applied to harmony, which I will briefly cover in the forthcoming sections. These concepts are addressed in detail in most music theory textbooks, but for now, it's enough to point out some basic concepts. If any of these concepts are confusing, you should seek out additional information to learn about tonal areas. There are several videos that are freely available through UreMusic.com that can help you learn about basic music theory concepts.

Classical period music tends to start with the tonic I chord, which gets embellished in various ways. Theorists refer to this embellishment area as the tonic area.

The goal of the tonic area is to reach the dominant of the key, which is the V chord that is built on the fifth scale degree of a major or minor work. To get to the V chord, common-practice composers often use the IV or II chord as a predominant. Other names for the predominant include the subdominant or dominant preparation.

The arrival of the IV or II chord signifies the predominant area, which then leads into the dominant area. When the tonic, predominant, or dominant chords serve to bring about a new tonal area or prepare a cadence, they are considered functional. When these chords embellish a tonal area without leading directly to the next tonal area, they are considered non-functional.

In the discussion of the tonic, predominant, and dominant chords, uppercase Roman numerals are used. It's implied that the II chord is minor in a major key and diminished in a minor key. The VII is diminished in major keys and diminished or major in minor keys.

The Phrase Model

The phrase model is a concept in music that is essentially tonal in nature. The phrase model consists of three or four areas, which are referred to as the tonic area, (predominant area), dominant area, and tonic closure. The predominant area is in parentheses because it is not always used in a musical work.

Composers of the classical and romantic period would often create phrases that are based on the phrase model. The tonic area typically starts with the tonic area, and then it introduces inversions of the I chord and other unstable chords to create a sense of forward motion. The forward motion often pulls back some with the introduction of the predominant chords. Sometimes, the predominant area is expanded as well. Finally, the predominant brings about the dominant for the key, which creates additional tension and a need to resolve back to the I chord. The V-I authentic cadence that comes at the end of so many pieces creates a powerful pull to signify the end of a phrase.

An example of the phrase model can be seen in the piece, "Kriegslied der Österreicher," by Ludwig van Beethoven. The tonic area is marked with a T below the first I chord. The predominant (PD) indicates a IV chord, and the dominant (D) indicates the V chord. Finally, it resolves to I in the tonic closure (T) in measure 4. Normally, a line would also be drawn from the start of the tonic area to the beginning of the predominant area to indicate an expansion.

Ludwig van Beethoven, "Kriegslied der Österreicher," WoO 122

Componirt im April 1797.

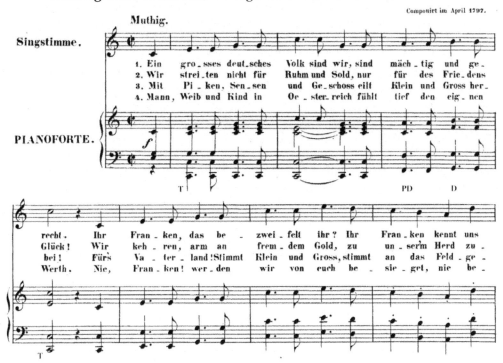

The phrase model is a complex concept that is explained in greater detail in *Craft of Music Composition*, which is the third volume of this series. It is enough right now to be introduced to the general concept of the phrase model. If you don't yet understand the concept of Roman numeral analysis, it's a good idea to take a basic music theory course; however, you will be able to continue through this textbook without an understanding of this concept.

The Tonic Chord

The I chord serves a functional role when it establishes the tonic or resolves the dominant. The I chord can serve a non-functional role when serving to expand one of the tonal areas – the tonic area, predominant area, dominant area, and tonic closure.

The Predominants

The IV and II chords often serve as predominants to the dominant, and when this happens, these chords are considered to be functional. Just like the I chord; they can exist solely in a non-functional way when they serve as expansions of tonal areas. Most commonly, these chords expand the tonic and predominant areas and not the dominant area.

The Dominants

The V or VII chord can serve a functional role as the dominant of the key in a classical work. These chords are only functional when they occur as a part of a cadence, which is the goal of a tonal phrase. The V chord can also serve a non-functional role when it serves only to expand a tonic area, predominant area, or even dominant area.

The manner in which chords can serve functional or non-functional roles can be illustrated more clearly using an example from tonal music. Consider the case of embellishing tones:

Passing tones (dissonant stepwise motion between two consonant harmony tones) can become defining characteristics of a motive to serve a functional role if the resulting dissonance is used in the same manner each time the motive appears. If the passing tone is just an elaboration of a motive, serves only to move between two notes without leaping, and doesn't recur consistently, then it is only serving a non-functional role.

If all this talk about chords and passing tones is confusing, the concept should become clear as you continue to read. Additionally, if you lack a theory background, the concept of functionality in relationship to harmony may not provide the best comparison for you. But don't despair, most of the text will explain the concept of functional and non-functional elements without the music theory jargon.

For now, just remember that a functional element serves a purpose, and it is not a mere decoration. A non-functional element is designed purely to decorate a piece and add interest.

Elements

"Composing is like playing with building blocks, continually making new buildings from the same old blocks."

~ Gustav Mahler

Gustav Mahler was a well-known composer of the Romantic period. He once remarked that composing was akin to working with building blocks. Elements serve as the building blocks of your composition. In some ways, you can think of motives as building blocks as well, but as you'll learn, they can be broken down into elements. Since motives can be broken down, it makes more sense to refer to elements as the most basic building blocks and motives as intermediate building blocks.

When you sit down to create a new composition, you're working with raw materials that developed throughout a piece. When you break down the music to its simplest state, music is the organized and (hopefully) intentional arrangement of both vertical and horizontal elements.

Elements are the worker bees of a composition. They don't always get much attention and acknowledgment for the final product, but they are essential to building the piece and holding everything together. When you are developing your motives, you should think about what elements are present. Aim to include at least two or three elements per motive to create better cohesion, but don't infuse every element available. Leaving some of the elements out makes it possible to modify, rebuild, and develop your motives as the piece develops.

When combining elements, it's essential to leave room for development. If your motives are too saturated with elements, then it will be hard to develop them because you've already set a precedent for your motive to include all elements. If your motive only consists of the elements of pitch, rhythm, and registral space, then you have some room to modify the dynamics and articulations in further iterations of the motive. The trick is to keep at least two elements the same every time the motive appears and then change the remaining elements in any way that makes sense to you. By doing this, you'll be able to create motives that always contain a common thread and develop in novel and cohesive ways.

While you are modifying the elements in your motives, it's important to remember that there is a difference between modification for the sake of modification and modification for the sake of creating an artistic and organic work. The rest of this chapter will discuss several kinds of elements that can be manipulated in a composition.

The following list contains some examples of elements:

Rhythm
Time signatures
Dynamics
Tempo
Pitch
Articulations
Slurs and Phrase Marks
Breath marks
Bar lines

Elements can contribute to a musical work in a variety of ways, and I've included a few examples to help get you on the right path:

- Without dynamics, monotony would begin to overtake the composition.
- Without pitch, a composition could not rise and fall.
- Without rhythm, the composition would stagnate and lack motion.
- Without registral space (a subset of pitch), individual instruments would not be able to take advantage of the differing timbres inherent as an instrument moves through its range.

Many apprentices and a number of practiced composers overlook things such as articulations, dynamics, and other score indications. Composers need to realize that these elements change entirely the interpretation of a composition. Without these elements, the performer doesn't have the information necessary to interpret a piece of music. This is unfair to the musicians that must put in the effort to learn to play a composition. When I was first starting out as a composer, I often kept this in mind. If it took a performer 12 hours to learn the music, then I felt I should spend at least twice that long editing.

Performers can't be expected to take a music composition seriously if it seems like the composer put minimal effort into the music. It's also worth noting that few professional composers completely ignore these elements. At the most basic level, a composition without performance indications is only partially complete. A simple *staccato* or *forte* marking can make all the difference in the final performance and interpretation of the work.

While traditional instruction in composition focuses on the tenets of music composition, many instructors fail to address the concept of using elements to build motives that can be torn apart and built up again in new ways throughout the development of a musical work. When a discussion of motives does occur, it's identified as the smallest complete musical idea without getting too deep into the other elements that make up a motive. We tend to look at motives as defined by nothing more than pitch and rhythm, but every aspect can have a relationship to the larger whole. This is what makes a piece coherent and learning to work with elements to build cornerstones offers a sort of system that doesn't lock a composer into any one genre.

Rhythm

Rhythm has a direct relationship to both the motives in a composition and the cornerstones of music composition. Without rhythm, motives would lack form. Music wouldn't be able to take on the illusion of movement through time, and the orchestration would lose a great deal of its power and emotive ability. Additionally, well-defined forms would not be possible without rhythm since most compositions require rhythm to create structure in a musical work.

Rhythm can imply harmony by creating a lasting connection or association with a motive or melody. When you hear a unique and readily identifiable rhythm that reuses the same harmony, the rhythm and harmony start to imply the existence of the other. If the rhythm occurs later in the music by itself without the harmony attached, the listener will still recall the association between the rhythm and its harmony. This relationship leads the listener to better identify the element and cornerstone as connected. Rhythm is an element that can significantly influence a composition. Think of rhythm as a driving force that provides momentum for a composition. Rhythm has the ability to propel the music forward or pull in on the reigns.

Composers should challenge themselves to think about unique ways to compose new rhythms and meet the challenge of creating original works. The process of creating simple rhythms often serves as a suitable remedy for overcoming writer's block since the creation of rhythm can spark the creative fire necessary to begin thinking about melody and harmony. Often what happens is that pitch naturally develops out of rhythm, and then these two elements begin to feed off each other.

Composers who have trouble creating vibrant rhythms may find that working through and practicing a book of rhythms can help them learn to write something innovative by introducing new and challenging music to learn and perform. Rhythm affects many aspects of a musical work, and it serves as a crucial element impacting progressions, climaxes, changes in mood, and tempo.

The Relevance of Rhythm in Music

Musical expression results from a combination of melody, rhythm, dynamics, and articulations that define how notes are attacked and released. Rhythm serves to provide the driving force behind a composition. Without rhythm, the pitch would float aimlessly in space, melodies wouldn't have a defined shape, and the music would lack features that make it memorable. It's possible to express rhythm on multiple levels – as an element that exists solely of rhythmic values or as a broad concept built in combination with several other elements.

Using Rhythm to Increase Tension

It's possible to increase the intensity of the rhythm by increasing its speed or complexity. These modifications can bring about a dramatic climax that pitch and dynamics alone could not create. Speed up a rhythm or use a more complex rhythm to increase anxiety and drama in a musical work. Slow it down to bring in a more passive, calm, or pastoral section.

Rhythm can affect the listener in profound ways, so it's critical to take time to work out any rhythms in a musical work. A good suggestion is to rework a rhythm at least three distinctive ways on different days of the week. Taking a break from work makes it possible to view the rhythm with fresh eyes and identify issues that weren't readily apparent upon the initial creation.

Using Rhythm to Introduce New Sections

The slowing down or speeding up of rhythm can be used to introduce new sections. Rhythms often don't establish themselves entirely at the beginning of a new section. Instead, rhythm commonly undergoes a development throughout the piece in a manner that is similar to how the melody develops. Exceptions to this general guideline exist, but composers should make sure there is a compelling reason to go against this natural tendency.

When an idea for a complete rhythm comes to mind, start by breaking that rhythm down into smaller pieces. Then, gradually join those pieces together over time until the piece climaxes in a grand revelation of the complete rhythm. Breaking apart the rhythm to create smaller elements that can be developed and reorganized is a great technique for developing musical ideas.

Time Signatures

The meter of the piece is expressed using a time signature. How to use a time signature is one of the first things you learn when you start to read music. The problem with meter is that so many composers tend to put in a time signature and then write the rest of the music like an automaton that refuses to recognize the time signature can be changed. The opposite also occurs when composers change the time signature every measure for no musical reason. It's important to use time signatures wisely and change only when the motive wants to do something different in the composition.

After selecting a time signature, it usually takes an assassin coming to the door and threatening composers with their life before they are willing to change the meter. I should harp on this some more. But you'll change the time signature appropriately in your rhythms without me reminding you, right? I hope so. Of course, you also shouldn't change the meter just for the sake of change. There should be a reason why your time signature is changing.

While I would love to give you some simple guidelines to follow for knowing when and how to change your time signature, you have to base it on how your motive develops and how you want it to change for functional purposes. Let's get esoteric for a moment. Ask yourself a question: what's more natural and likely to occur in the wild?

1.   A cat who always moves at the same pace. It never speeds up, slows down, or steps in a new direction. Essentially, a cat that is a robot.

2.   A cat who is silent one moment and then lashing out at the invisible visitor/ghost in the next. An erratic dash most likely follows as the cat speeds through the house and annihilates your flowers.

The correct answer is No. 2. If your cat acts like the example in No. 1, it's an imposter. Your real cat created a robot in exquisite likeness to distract you and throw you off guard. Don't say I didn't warn you. If you answered No. 1, you have a cat problem that you should deal with before continuing.

It's possible to learn a lot from nature. There are very few living, organic creatures in nature that move and react in a highly predictable way. They have their minds and instincts, and even something as simple as changing the environment shapes how they react. Your compositions should do the same. If your motive transforms, why can't your time signature? Of course, you can break any theory you want when you're composing original music, and the assumption that time signature changes are an excellent way to add interest is just a theory. Still, you should have a reason for making any change.

Nature is repetitive, but it a very subtle and beautiful way. Trees may fill a forest, but now two trees are going to be exactly the same. Philip Glass is a 20th/21st century composer who writes in a style of musical known as minimalism. He is the King of Repetition. He makes repetition work by carefully balancing minuscule changes. This kind of composing takes time to learn, and it can be difficult to employ effectively. By learning the rules before breaking them, you will have a better understanding of why you are making compositional choices.

The concept of musical development applies to time signatures. Time signatures are not these immovable devices that must never change. To develop your technique, you should be flexible enough to change your time signatures and gain familiarity working with asymmetrical rhythms.

When the time signature changes, your rhythm may also change. It's crucial to pick the time signature that fits your rhythm. For that reason, I'm going to spend a bit of time talking about time signatures. After all, if you plan on composing or playing music, you should have a healthy respect for time signatures.

I should start by saying that yes, it can be difficult to tell the time signature used in a musical work; however, this is where a knowledge of musical time periods and conventional compositional devices come in handy. In specific time periods, composers were more likely to prefer particular time signatures.

In the classical period, there is a concept known as real and notated measures. Real measures are what we hear, and notated measures are what we see written in the notation. In the classical period, there is a theory that most phrases are 4 measures long. This means that a piece in 2/4 may have an 8-measure phrase, but it will sound to the listener as a 4-measure phrase. The concept of real vs. notated measures is supported by theorists like William E. Caplin. In fact, time periods often have a dramatic impact on the manner that a piece is performed. Stylistic differences for each time signature were also inferred by the time period. The common practice largely dictated the choices made. Usually, you can identify the right time signature if you recognize the musical style and have a good grasp of music history.

The progression of a musical work is another factor that influences the time signature. If you're only given a brief 8-measure melody to work with, then it's not always possible to tell the time signature. The best you can do is make a very close educated guess.

Choosing the Right Time Signature

So, here is the big question. How can you tell the difference between music written in 2/4 and 2/2 time or 3/8 and 3/4 time? Let's assume that a master composer wrote the piece, and the composer chose a time signature for a particular reason.

In case you missed that, there is an implication here that composers who don't know what they're doing might not choose the best time signature (and some of them are very successful at being clueless). Just because a musical work is in print doesn't mean the composer wrote it in the best way possible. Many talented composers fail to use the most effective time signature for their works. Choosing the wrong time signature isn't necessarily a reflection of their talent as a composer. Still, it may preclude them from getting a commission or receiving a performance from a well-known conductor.

Let's take a look at one of the most famous symphonies of all time – Beethoven's Fifth Symphony. If you aren't familiar with this work, listen to a performance. I'm sure you'll quickly recognize the melody.

Here are a few details you should be able to see clearly:

- The opening rhythm contains three eighths followed by a half note.
- The time signature is 2/4.
- The pulse occurs on the first beat, and it includes a weaker second beat. This information is made clear by the time signature that is employed.
- There is a weak measure followed by a strong measure structure in every other measure. (This is a concept known as hypermeter.)

Would it make sense to write the opening in a 4/8-time signature? In this case, no, because the division of the beat (pulse) in 2/4 time emphasizes the quarter note and not the eighth note. If the composer chose 4/8 time, we might hear the piece as having four separated beats since the eighth note is the value of the beat.

If written in 4/4 time, and quarter notes were used instead of eighth notes, then it wouldn't have the lilting quality of 2/4 since there would be a multi-level emphasis of the beat structure. Remember, in 2/4 time, the structure of the beats is typically strong-weak or strong-medium. In 4/4 time, it's strong-weak, medium-weakest.

Since this piece is in 2/4 time, the eighth note is considered the subdivision for the composition. That means the structure of the beat is strong-weak, where the eighth notes on the offbeat (after the strong and the weak quarter notes) are considered equally balanced in terms of accent. Even if we changed the time signature to 4/4, and we changed the note values from eighth notes to quarter notes, the structure would have a different strong-weak-medium-weaker structure, where the offbeats would use a weak-weaker structure in contrast to the weak-weak offbeat structure of 2/4.

We hear those eighth notes in the beginning as being grouped into one continuous series of notes with a slight emphasis on beat two, and strangely, we "hear" an accent of silent anticipation on the strong first beat even though there is a rest. Beethoven creates tension with a rest by repeating this figure, and the audience practically holds their breath on that first beat because the anticipation of the offbeat is so intense.

So, we know that in 2/4 time, there is a strong beat followed by a weak beat. Beat one is the strong beat and beat two is the weak beat. Unless the composer includes an accent on one of the beats, the first beat of the measure should be emphasized more strongly than the second.

Any time signature that has a four on the bottom tells you that the quarter note should be held for one beat (pulse).

While you can't hear a time signature, you can feel the pulse. When you listen to the Beethoven piece, it should be clear that the pulse is the quarter note and not the eighth note. You might even hear the pulse as the half note if the performers don't slightly accent the second eighth note in each measure. While a computer would likely play 4/8 and 4/4 similarly, composers and performers should be intentional about the nuances inferred from time signatures.

Try clapping the rhythmic motive in 2/4 time. The first time you perform the rhythm, clap the rhythm with the emphasis on the quarter note beats and the eighth notes as a fluidly connected set of two beats. So, the first eighth note will act as a weaker "pickup" into the eighth note that falls on the beat.

Now try clapping the rhythm as if it were in 4/8 with a strong first beat emphasis, a weaker second beat emphasis, a medium third beat emphasis, and make the fourth beat the weakest beat. It just doesn't sound the same. In 4/8 time, the eighth notes have a different accent structure. 4/4 time may sound similar to 4/8 time, but even with these similar time signatures, a piece played in 4/4 time has less separation between the notes than one played in 4/8 time. Quarter notes imply a longer and sustained note compared to eighth notes.

In 2/4 time, the first and last eighth notes of the measure will sound with the same approximate accent structure. In 4/8 time, the first eighth note would have a stronger accent than the last. If you combined the first two measures into one measure so that measures 1 and 2 occurred in one 4/4 measure, then the downbeat on the half note would lose some of its force and stability since it would happen on a semi-weak beat in 4/4 time instead of a strong beat in 2/4 time.

You can generally narrow down the type of time signature by paying attention to the phrasing and determining how the composer would most likely write the piece. The other option is to look at the score. Since the score is your responsibility to create, you don't have this luxury.

Demonstration of beat structure in various time signatures. Try performing all of these rhythms using the accent structure provided.

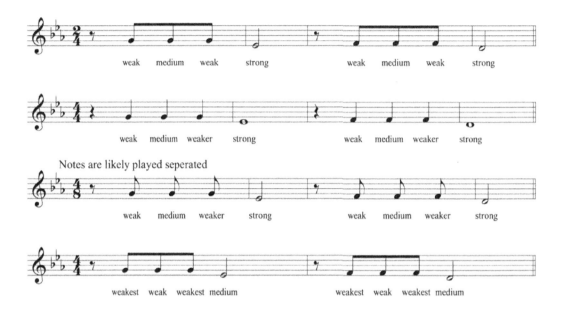

Guidelines for Selecting the Right Time Signature

As a composer, you are responsible for making sure your music is playable. In the case of 2/4 and 4/8, there may not be apparent clues to indicate the correct time signature. However, there is still often a good and better time signature to use. There will usually be one option that is more elegant than its alternatives.

Some Basic Principles to Follow:

- **Listen to the phrasing.** Does the music imply a pulse repeating at a regularly recurring interval?
- **Listen to the grouping of notes.** If they sound separated, chances are you're dealing with a time signature that emphasizes the separation of the notes and has a pulse on each main beat.
- **Consider the performer.** Would the piece be more natural to perform in 4/4 time or 4/8 time? If the piece is slow, then 4/4 time generally makes the most sense. If the piece is faster, then 4/8 time might be the best option. Readability is always a factor.
- **Consider the conductor.** Is there a time signature that would make it easier for the conductor? A swift march in 4/4 may be impractical for a conductor to conduct every beat, but a 2/2 (cut-time) time signature could make more sense.

Ultimately, you have to pick the time signature that works best for the piece. It's essential to take some time to evaluate the time signature and make sure it makes sense for your music. Think about how the accents fall naturally in each time signature and consider ways you can throw in an unexpected twist with some complex (irregular) time signatures like 5/4, 9/4, or 5/8.

Of course, you also may decide that time signatures are out of style, as Messiaen did in his composition, *Quartet for the End of Time*.

Dynamics

Dynamics accentuate the musical form and give motives shape. They can be used to enhance critical musical elements and serve as guideposts along the way to promote the development of the composition. Dynamics are one of the most basic requirements for most compositions, but composers often don't know the best places to put them. In general, the beginning of the piece, new sections, and the top and bottom of a climax are appropriate places to consider whether a dynamic change is warranted. Other possible places include the beginning and end of phrases when you need to indicate a shift in mood or a subtle change in the interpretation. You can also use dynamics to soften an aggressive line or make a lyrical line agitated in nature. Carefully choose your dynamics and make sure they add to the piece or help to clarify the mood of a section. There are few things more distracting than the composer who puts an articulation or dynamic marking on every single note in a piece.

Carefully placed dynamic crescendos (a gradual increase in volume) can produce highly competent, dramatic, and emotional moments in a composition. Decrescendos (a gradual decrease in volume) can relieve or create tension depending on the context of the music. Dynamics may be used to make background parts less prominent, but this should be employed carefully. Performers are naturally going to bring out the melodic elements, so you don't need to indicate the melody by using a louder dynamic. However, in some cases, you may use two dynamics for two different parts if one part is radically different than the other. One example of this is when one part is intended to act as a background accompaniment and not a primary musical device.

Crescendos and decrescendos are also crucial in helping to articulate climaxes and the edges of phrases. These can be used to provide more dimension to music and improve the overall sound and feel of the composition. When appropriately used, dynamics can also serve a functional role. Aim to employ dynamics sparingly since too many dynamics can cause information overload and may make the composition impractical to perform.

Improper Use of Dynamics

Dynamics are used to help articulate the form of a piece and the shape of melodies and rhythms. In general, composers have avoided the use of dynamics in certain instances where dynamics aren't appropriate or essential. This section outlines some of the methods a composer uses to write music with dynamics. Following these guidelines results in more productive rehearsals and less time spent preparing a piece for performance.

Relative Dynamics

Some composers will write a flute with a *forte* marking while the trumpet is simultaneously playing *piano*. They do this because the flute is not as penetrating as the trumpet, so they want it to stand out. It makes logical sense, but it is confusing to both the conductor and the ensemble. It is better to write the overall ensemble dynamic for all parts. If there is a solo part, a louder dynamic marking may make sense. Even in this case, a solo marking informs the performer to come through the texture and play louder than the ensemble. Marking a solo part also makes it easier for the conductor to find the main melodic line in a concert score. In general, if a passage is meant to use a particular dynamic, then all the parts should be marked the same way.

Counterintuitive Dynamics

Don't forget that music follows some basic protocols when ascending and descending. Even students who practice their musical scales will naturally increase volume toward the top of a scale and decrease the volume on the way down. If you're not practicing your scales this way on your primary instrument, you should try it to develop your concept of dynamic range. Keep this natural dynamic tendency in mind when writing dynamics in your music.

Counterintuitive dynamics are employed when the goal is to change the perception of a melodic line. When playing scales, it's naturel to increase in volume as the performer ascends and decrease in volume during the descent. This natural rise and fall is an example of intuitive dynamics. Reverse the tendency by decreasing in volume toward the top of the scale and the dynamics become counterintuitive.

Using dynamic markings correctly can have a dramatic effect on the performance of a work. Avoid counterintuitive actions that go against the natural tendency of the melody unless careful consideration is paid to determine why it is necessary, and if the end justifies the means required to accomplish the goal. It's often possible to find straightforward and elegant solutions, and the goal should be to use dynamics to enhance the music. Sometimes, a little bit of thought is all that is required to determine an adequate solution.

Generally, you should avoid writing counterintuitive dynamics. Don't make the performer play softly in an extremely high tessitura. Avoid increasing the volume at the end of a phrase. Create reasonable expectations and don't expect the ensemble to reduce the overall volume if you add more instruments. Of course, there are exceptions to every rule, especially if the descent is a fall into something fiery and dramatic and a *fortissimo* is warranted. However, following basic guidelines result in a composition that is intuitive to perform.

Unrealistic Dynamics

If a composition requires that the lead trumpet player produces a high concert C5 above the staff, they shouldn't be expected to play it quietly unless they are an advanced player. Of course, there are plenty of outstanding performers who could play a high C at a *piano* dynamic marking with little difficulty. Still, consider the level of the ensemble and soloist when making these decisions.

Look at the piece as a whole to determine the overall difficulty level. If the piece requires a professional group, then the high tessitura and low dynamic in the trumpet should work fine. If the music is otherwise extremely accessible and playable, it doesn't make sense to limit the performance options by making one part significantly more complicated than the rest of the composition. The best way to learn what's possible is by talking with performers and hearing completed works rehearsed.

If the piece is mostly accessible, using another instrument that can comfortably play high without having to go against the natural tendencies of the instrument is probably the best alternative. To obtain a brassy sound, the combination of flute on the upper octave and a cornet an octave below offers another solution. Get creative with orchestrations to find the best resolution, but most importantly, get an orchestration text and start studying. You should also listen to as many performances as possible.

When in doubt, a composer should err on the side of caution. I am aware that this advice flies in the face of what many other instructors would tell a student. Often, instructors tell you to worry about the music and let the performer worry about the performance. However, I think this often makes a piece more difficult than needed, which can result in a poor or limited performance. Some musical works are difficult by nature, and that's perfectly fine. Whenever possible, I believe it makes more sense to write characteristically for the instrument so that the performer can concentrate on the music and not their technique.

Knowing the capabilities of each instrument is a subject area known as instrumentation, and instrumentation is a crucial part of any composer's training. Instrumentation courses teach composers about the range and clarifies problem areas for various instruments. Another related field is orchestration, where the composer learns about suitable instrument substitutions and instrument combinations.

Awkward Placement

A composer might place a *subito piano* marking right in the middle of a challenging sixteenth-note passage that is to be played at light speed and with more flares than a J.J. Abrams movie. It's challenging to perform this kind of impossible writing, so it's essential to be realistic about the dynamic employed. One possible solution is to give the part to a new player at the moment where it becomes suddenly quiet, direct them to start softly and then continue the line.

Avoid placing considerable crescendos in melodies that lack room for the performer to breathe. Wind performers must breathe, and when there is no room to breathe, they may cut notes and phrases short. Not many wind players know how to circular breathe, and it shouldn't be a requirement for them to play a musical work, unless the goal of the work is to be highly virtuosic.

Remember, this text isn't discussing how to write music that shows off a performer. Rather, this text focuses on how to create music that is natural and organic. Because of this, some of the suggestions won't apply to all types of music.

Often, performers will take a breath in a place that the composer may not find desirable if performance indications are missing. Composers who write long melodies without breaks usually include breath marks so that the performer does not have to second-guess the intentions. If the phrase has rests and pauses, then breath marks are typically not needed. The exception to this is if you have some larger formal goal that requires musicians to think of rest as part of the phrase.

Performers who have to work too hard to divine a composer's intentions might not enjoy playing the music. Failing to give the performer everything they need to play a piece well also takes away valuable rehearsal time that could be used to prepare a musical work.

Proper Use of Dynamics

There are plenty of ways to use dynamics effectively. Composers often learn to use dynamics through trial and error. Composers who do not play an instrument are going to have a more difficult time knowing when to include appropriate dynamic markings so it's a good idea to learn to play the piano or a string instrument if you don't yet play an instrument. The piano is useful for playing chords and working through your musical ideas. Meanwhile, string instruments are valuable instruments to play if you want to write for orchestra since all composers need to understand how to write effectively for strings.

Climactic Emphasis

Along with rhythm and pitch, dynamics are one of many ways to create a climactic moment in a musical work. Dynamics can be used to support the apex of a piece by raising the volume level through the highest point of the melody. By starting softly and increasing the volume towards a climax, it's possible to create a more intense swell. In combination with rhythm and pitch levels, it's possible to create very powerful climaxes with the right dynamics. In general, the highest note of the piece is usually coupled with the loudest dynamic marking. If a fortissimo is the loudest dynamic and repeatedly used throughout the music, it's time to evaluate the composition to find the primary climax and adjust the remaining dynamics around the peak.

Entrances

Each time a performer enters after a rest, you may need to include the dynamic marking. Even if it is the same dynamic as the previous phrase, it is sometimes essential to let the performer know the appropriate dynamic level.

If you're not an extremely famous composer, then you need to give the performer some clues to help them perform your work. Performers know how to play Mozart and Beethoven because numerous musicians have presented their music, and their styles have become familiar. Experience and a history of performances with a work gives performers context to understand how to interpret the music. Modern composers vary significantly in their preferred method, and there isn't a predominant modern style of writing. Because new music doesn't have a long history of performances, it makes it essential to give the performers adequate performance markings to interpret and perform a composition effectively.

Mood, Character, and Meaning

A composition that is marked *forte* is generally going to be boisterous, energetic, majestic, or proud. For this reason, the screaming *fortissimo* lullaby has not yet gained traction in mainstream music. Composers must make sure that the dynamics of the music reflects the current mood of the composition. Changing a dynamic level can instantly change how a section of music is perceived. A piece played with a *forte* dynamic may sound aggressive. That same section played at *piano* may take on an air of sadness or thoughtfulness. Beginning composers often get caught up in the notes and forget that the dynamics play a significant role in the performance and interpretation of a work.

Dynamics can drastically change the meaning of a motive, melody, or section of a piece. Even if the pitch and rhythmic material are the same, the meaning can change with a simple dynamic adjustment. An energetic motive from the beginning of a piece can suddenly seem fragile, soft, or sullen when dynamics change. Using dynamics to transform a piece that is scary or sad into something thoughtful or peaceful can often be accomplished by varying dynamics.

Creating Tension

Composers create subtle increases in tension by gradually intensifying the dynamics. Tension naturally increases as the dynamics get louder, and tension decreases as the dynamics get softer. Composers aim to avoid losing the listener's interest by incorporating more than one dynamic level. Compositions that use only one or two dynamics and never change tend to create tedious music.

Of course, there are exceptions to the dynamic guideline of increasing tension. While tension is often increased with louder dynamics, it's also possible to effectively create tense moments by lessening the dynamics. It depends on the nature of the melody, but in most cases, an increase in dynamics will also generate an increase in tension and vice versa.

Enhancing the Form

Dynamics can also enhance the form. If you have a simple A–B–A form, you could use different dynamics in both the A and the B sections. The different dynamics help emphasize the start of new sections. Perhaps the A sections use a *piano* dynamic level, and the B section is a bit louder at *mezzo forte*. Using dynamics in this way helps to clarify and define the form.

Tempo

Elements can be used to support the tempo of a piece. If a piece is *Maestoso*, then the composer would likely need to include a robust dynamic marking such as *mezzo forte*, *forte*, or *fortissimo*. If the piece is *Adagio*, then it is most likely that the dynamic level will be *piano* or *mezzo piano*. Composers should strive to avoid writing dynamics that are counterintuitive to the tempo marking. Writing dynamic markings that match the tempo results in a more effective and sensible piece that both audiences and performers can learn to appreciate.

When thinking about how to use tempo as an element, it's essential to consider how the musical line will change based on a tempo adjustment. If a composer writes a regal and slow opening motive and then reintroduces the motive at a later point in the composition, then it might make sense to change the tempo with the reintroduction of the motive. However, if the tempo changes, it might be necessary also to change the octave register where the original motive appears. A faster tempo might see the original motive played up an octave.

One way to use tempo as a functional element is to create a tempo that is so different from the rest of the piece that the tempo is immediately recognized when it comes back later. By doing this, it's possible to use a completely different melody, but bring it in at the original tempo. The audience will perceive that this new melody is related to the original tempo, but only if done correctly with good taste.

Like dynamics, adjusting the tempo to make it a functional rather than a non-functional element is exceptionally tricky. To complete this successfully, it makes sense to include more than one element to reinforce the tempo element and create greater coherence.

The tempo of your music will determine the mood it sets, and it determines the rate and speed of the pulse. It should be clear that when the tempo accelerates, the rate of the pulse also increases. Slow it down, and the pulse also slows down. Tempo often serves as an intrinsic part of the rhythm that can't be separated.

If you're a beginner, think of the pulse as the beat in music. It's the part of the music that makes us move and react physically. We may tap our feet in response to the music, or we may feel like clapping our hands or bobbing our heads. The pulse occurs regularly, and it acts as the motor that determines the rate that the music unfolds and develops. Time signatures and the rhythm often dictate the pulse.

There are a few ways that you can indicate the tempo of a piece. Composers in the seventeenth century used terms like *Andante, Allegro,* and *Presto* to show an approximate pace for the piece while also implying a particular mood. In the nineteenth century, composers started to get specific and control-freaky about their compositions. Composers added diminutives to the ends of these broad and general tempo markings. (Obviously, this was done to teach those seventeenth-century hacks a lesson.)

Instead of a perfectly fine *Andante,* you suddenly had tempo markings like *Andantino.* While *Andante* reflected an approximate pace of about 76 beats per minute with a somewhat casual walking feel, *Andantino* indicated the pace was to be just a little bit faster and lighter. My favorite tempo marking is *Andante con moto,* which essentially means "slowly with motion."

As if turning the world of tempo upside down with these new and more specific tempos weren't enough, these composers also started to use tempo indicators to express how to perform a musical work.

- *Andante con moto* indicates to perform music with a higher level of energy, and translates to "going, with motion."
- *Andante cantabile* suggests performing music in a singing style.
- *Andante rubato* is a beautiful way to screw up a musician's sense of reality. It essentially translates to, "it's all about the soloist so fasten yourself in because the steady and regular pulse that you've come to know and love is dead."

The tempo is important. It changes how rhythm is perceived, and it can turn a lovely, friendly ostinato into a race on the devil's chariot.

Tempo Marking List

The following list contains some of the most commonly used tempo markings. Aim to use this list in your compositions so that you can begin to become familiar with the different markings. Note that BPM stands for beats per minute. When the tempo marking ends with "-issimo", the tempo is generally increased. Adding an "-ino" or "-etto" ending tends to decrease the tempo. While the BPM indications below are conventional, the actual tempo may be a bit faster or slower.

- *Larghissimo* – extremely slow (22 bpm)
- *Grave* – very slow (23 –45 bpm)
- *Largo* – broadly (38 –60 bpm)
- *Lento* – slowly (43 –62 bpm)
- *Larghetto* – rather broadly (60 –66 bpm)
- *Adagio* – slow and stately (literally translates to "at ease") (64 –76 bpm)
- *Adagietto* – slower than andante (72 –76 bpm)
- *Andante* – at a walking pace (74 –108 bpm)
- *Andantino* – (usually) slightly faster than Andante (80 –108 bpm)
- *Marcia moderato* – moderately, in a march style (83 –85 bpm)
- *Andante moderato* – the middle road of andante and moderato (87 –112 bpm)
- *Moderato* – moderately (108 –124 bpm)
- *Allegretto* – moderately fast (112 –120 bpm)
- *Allegro moderato* – almost allegro (116 –124 bpm)
- *Allegro* – fast, quickly, and bright (120 –168 bpm)
- *Vivace* – lively and fast (168 –178 bpm)
- *Vivacissimo* – very fast and lively (172 –178 bpm)
- *Allegrissimo* or *Allegro vivace* – very fast (172 –180 bpm)
- *Presto* – very, very fast (168 –212 bpm)
- *Prestissimo* – even faster than Presto (212 bpm+)

Pitch

Pitches can exist without a clearly established rhythm in a musical work; but without rhythm, the pitches in music have no legs to move. While it's challenging to create motives that don't include both pitch and rhythm, one possibility is to play specific tones on an instrument with no regard to how much time has passed. This practice can be a meditative and tranquil experience. Merely sitting at an instrument and randomly playing pitches with no rhythm or sense of time can promote a deeply relaxing session, but it's difficult to employ in a musical work.

Pitch refers simply to the highness or lowness of a sound. There are many factors to contemplate when considering pitch elements, including the timbre, placement, alterations, and the registral space of the pitch.

Pitch Alteration

One of the most exciting ways to use pitch is to select specific rhythmic elements within a melody and to change them subtly, which creates a natural sense of growth and change. In this way, it is possible to create a composition that begins to develop organically. By keeping the rhythm the same and only changing pitch, you can create some really incredible transformations in your composition.

Composers who find themselves constantly repeating their ideas verbatim must find ways to change these ideas subtly. Even in specific genres where it is idiomatic to repeat certain key elements, it's possible to make subtle changes that breathe new life into the work while still maintaining a trance-like and meditative pulse in the background. Put a subtle twist on each further recurrence of an idea to discover how making small modifications enhance the piece by making it vibrant and three-dimensional. This basic modification technique should be in every composer's toolkit.

Composers must be aware of how the modification of pitch affects the overall mood of the line. When there is an essentially major-mode line, a composer would likely avoid suddenly lowering the third of a major chord unless they wanted to invoke that minor mode. Composers can create more elegant and subtle modifications by slowing introducing the idea of a switch to the minor key.

Consider the process of modulating to a new key. A quick way to get to a new key involves the use of pivot chords and direct modulations. Essentially, a pivot chord occurs when you choose a chord that fits in more than one key while a direct modulation may simply move dramatically into the new key.

On an even more basic and intuitive level, you can also modify select pitches from a scale. Gradually progress from major to minor by first lowering the sixth scale degree and alternating between a lowered and raised sixth. Make the modulation final by lowering the third scale degree and use a cadence that announces the new minor key. Changing the individual pitches in a piece will affect the overall musical line, and it's critical to understand how to manipulate pitch to create interesting music.

Composers must be experts in the avoidance of changes that would make a composition awkward or create modulations that seem out of place. In modulations, the trick is to slowly introduce pitches from the new key into the piece while using the underlying chords to change the structure of the piece from one key into another new key. Most modulations should occur over several measures. Similar to foreshadowing techniques in literature, introduce a modulation with a few of the pitches from the new key interspersed before the big drive to land in the new territory.

Music theory often teaches non-direct modulations using pivot chords and applied (secondary) chords. In actual music, this is rarely how a modulation occurs. While these techniques can help take a piece into a new key center, they often result in abrupt, awkward, and unmusical solutions. Composers should plan to create a modulation that takes at least four measures to reach its goal.

A technique similar to modulation is a tonicization. But in a tonicization, the music doesn't leave the primary key center. Instead, the tonicization briefly moves into a new key and quickly returns. Tonicizations are usually created by employing dominants from a nearby key to create a more impactful dominant-tonic cadence in tonal music. Of course, depending on the theory camp you're coming from, you also may believe that modulations don't exist and everything is a tonicization.

Instrument Timbre

Instrument timbre changes the color of musical elements and adds definition to the cornerstones of composition, including melody, form, texture, harmony, orchestration, and counterpoint. Instrument timbre refers to the timbre associated with each instrument and not the mechanics of instrument capabilities. Using instrument timbre as an element requires the composer to use instruments in a functional role that creates the sound of the piece.

Conventional instruction often views timbre as unrelated to the development of a motive, but it's linked intimately with pitch. And the placement of the pitches in a piece will affect the overall timbre of a composition. Additionally, timbre can be used to create a very easily identifiable functional element within a composition. For example, if an oboe only comes in to play a solo, that oboe line is now serving a functional role because the audience will recognize the oboe solo as a recurring element. The oboe could come in on entirely different melodies, but the character of the timbre will create a link between these melodies. I realize this may raise some objections, but only if you forget the underlying principle of combining at least two elements consistently throughout a composition to create a motive. If you always combine two elements in the same way, and freely change the remaining elements, the piece will have coherence.

The octave register employed affects the timbre of the instrument and pitch, and by merely lowering the pitch an octave, the sound can become dense and gritty. Composers must think about the register of the pitch to pick the right register for the desired effect. This concept is explained more in the discussion of registral space, but composers must realize the importance of the pitch register in a musical work. Pitches played in a higher register are going to sound much different than pitches played in a lower register. This is partially due to the limits of our hearing. Higher pitches have fewer overtones that can be heard, and they can sound shriller as a result.

At this point, I'm going to diverge a moment to talk about an important issue. Students of harmony learn the most common way to connect chords based on the works of the most famous composers. They also learn the most common progression of harmonies that were used by a group of composers. If a student follows the guidelines, they will create a progression that has no faults other than the fact that the harmony will lack creativity. The principle of combining elements to create cohesion follows this same critical premise. Just because two elements are combined, and that creates cohesion, it does not mean the composer has created artful cohesion. Musical taste still has to be developed to make a piece both coherent and comprehensible, and that can only be accomplished through refining the ear, listening to music, learning the tenets, and having a certain degree of talent and aptitude for music.

Articulations

Articulations modify the attack or release of a pitch and effect the melody, harmony, or texture. Composers can disrupt the standard beat structure of a composition using articulations. For example, a piece with no articulations in 4/4 time would use a strong-weak-medium-weakest (or weaker in relation to the weak beat) structure. Pay attention to the natural accents inherent in each time signature, and use articulations to emphasize, de-emphasize, or obliterate the natural accent structure.

The articulations used in a particular section can have a dramatic effect on how the piece is perceived. A heavy accent can instill a sense of urgency or a commanding presence. A tenuto mark can soften a section and make it more subdued. As with dynamic markings, articulations are just as important as the pitches. Articulations can turn what would otherwise be a normal common time signature with four beats per measure into a piece that sounds like it was written in 7/8 time. By obscuring the natural beat with articulations, a composer can temporarily disrupt the rhythm of a composition.

Articulations also affect the pitch by changing the timbre of the instrument. A harsh accent may make a trumpet sound brassy and aggressive. While a soft accent can make the trumpet sound mellow and relaxed. Down-bows and up-bows on a string instrument affect the way the audience perceives an entrance. Articulations are essential to the interpretation of a musical line. They can even serve a functional role in a piece where a strong accent can mark key points in a musical work. However, for the accent to stand out, the surrounding pitches must use dramatically different articulations.

Registral Space

The term registral space refers to the register where a particular note, instrument, or ensemble plays. For example, C4 (middle C) to G4 could constitute one area of registral space. C5 to G5 could represent another. When composers place instruments into their own confined registral space, and then include a small gap between the different registers, the instruments become more pronounced. Registral space is essentially the space that a particular segment of pitches occupies. A composition written in the highest register of the violin would be considered to occupy a high registral space. Stated simply, registral space refers to a range of notes in the musical register.

Instruments each have their own range of pitches that they can produce. This results in a type of registral space where instruments that use a similar range and timbre are grouped together. This isolation of instrument groups makes them more pronounced since different ensembles exist in different registral spaces. When you take range in tandem with timbre, the isolation becomes even more pronounced. Brass and woodwind groups have dramatically different sounds even though they can often play in the same registral space. However, if you place the woodwinds an octave above the brass, the differentiation between the groups becomes more apparent as the woodwinds serve as an outline for the brass section. Place the brass and woodwinds in the same registral space, and they begin to blend and combine timbres.

The registral space of instrument ensembles serves as one of the principles of orchestration. The orchestra consists of instruments that all occupy different registral spaces. The violins and flutes share an area, the trombones and bassoons share a space, and the tubas and cellos share a space. These different registers will not only have an impact on the overall form of the composition, but they will also sound different because of the octave register and timbre.

The rhythm element may provide the driving force and act as the motor that pushes the composition forward, but it's the element of pitch that makes it possible to create registral space in a composition. Imagine a work where the flutes, oboes, and clarinets perform at the top of their range in close spacing while the low brass reside in the lower octave of their limits. This separation of pitches by multiple octaves creates a sense of registral space that allows the listener to identify the contrasting elements of a composition. Registral space makes the instrumental differences between the woodwinds and brass even more pronounced.

Registral space is one of the most exciting aspects of music, and it has specific new relevance in the age of computers. With computers, it is now possible to create spaces that are even more dramatic. The composer may write a French horn emanating from the back of the room, while flutes manifest from the front of the hall. It's also possible to make the instrument sound as if it's flying through the room as the sound is panned through several speakers.

With a complete surround sound system, music has the capability of existing all around the listener, which also makes it easier to hear the different instruments. An audience member can turn to the left to listen to the strings and face the front to listen to the flutes. Imagine creating the illusion of a particular instrument moving in circles around the listener. To truly understand this, recall an experience in a movie theater. Listen to the sound effects, and it will become apparent that the sound comes from all around the theater. While it would be humorous to see a live performance with musicians being wheeled around the room to create these effects, this sort of movement of sound is only feasible with the use of computers and an elaborate speaker setup.

Registral space is essentially just a term used to describe the pitch range that an individual or group of instruments occupies. A piece could open with a small section that occupies a single register. The work could then expand to include the entire registral space of the orchestra. Registral space can refer to the location from which a particular sound emanates in addition to its octave register.

Cornerstones

Cornerstones are the large-scale parts that require one or more elements or motives to function. A proper definition of the term cornerstone is "an important quality or feature on which a particular thing depends or is based." Some cornerstones require the combination of more elements than other cornerstones. Still, the concept of a cornerstone is essential to the philosophy of music composition proposed in this primer on creating music.

When a composer reaches a certain level of mastery, they can compose a pure motive and know approximately how long the piece will be and what kind of form the work will require. Developing the level of mastery to foresee the length and breadth of a musical work comes only with time and experience. It's the difference between a composer who is at the beginning stages and a composer who has the skill and ability to navigate the creation of a musical work expertly.

A younger composer tends to write the story as they go, but the master composer generally knows from the *germ of an idea* how the piece will unfold before setting a note to the paper. For an advanced composer, the process of composing may involve rehearsing a piece internally in their mind, and then nailing down the final details and making edits for performance and practicality after notating the work in its entirety. The melodic, contrapuntal, orchestral, and harmonic outline of the composition exists in near totality before setting a single note to the paper.

Cornerstones are much too broad of a concept to discuss in detail in a book of this nature. Instead of providing a crash course in cornerstones, I suggest you seek out established books that deal with the cornerstones of music theory, counterpoint, orchestration, and form. By doing so, you will be able to come back to this textbook and apply the concept of elements and cornerstones to your work.

Phrase

The melody or phrase is one of the main features of a composition. Several phrases may result in the creation of periods. The period is traditionally made up of two or more smaller phrases known as the antecedent and consequent phrase. Combine a few phrases or periods, and a section of music forms. Smaller elements combine to create melodies, which ultimately leads to the creation of a musical work.

Melody can mean different things depending on the time period and the composer in question. Several modern pieces obliterate and redefine the concept of a melody. In contemporary music, a melody can be anything from a short collection of notes to *Klangfarbenmelodie*, where the melody gets split between several different instruments. Typically, melodies stem from one or more motives that are combined to create the structure of the melody.

In most musical styles, it's generally agreed that motives create melodies. (Remember that motives are composed of smaller elements, including pitch, rhythms, dynamics, articulations, and timbre.) Melodies can often be described by referring to their contour. A melody could be abstractly described as undulating, arching, falling, rising, angular, or erratic.

Change any single element of a melody, and there is a good chance that the melody will still sound recognizable to the listener if you keep at least two elements intact within a single motive. Composers modify their melodies throughout a musical work to create change and dramatically alter a piece.

Changing one element of the melody and replacing it with another is one method composers use to develop a piece. By changing only one element, such as pitch, while keeping at least one other element the same, a melody can retain its relationship to the original melody. Composers walk a fine line between changing too many elements and not changing enough elements to keep a piece of music driving forward. Keeping all of the elements the same and failing to make changes to any elements in a melody usually results in stagnation.

A composition that uses more than one element consistently in a melody while modifying and changing other elements plants the seeds of an organic musical work. Composers go to great pains to create melodies that have all the necessary elements to create a much larger work. A theme that doesn't lend itself well to change will necessarily result in a shorter musical work.

Voice Leading

Voice leading can be a complicated subject; however, learning the rules of voice leading will help you to create compelling compositions. Proper voice leading can make a highly dissonant section in music seem less jarring to the listener. Voice leading can smooth over nearly any chord progression and make it sound balanced and effortless to the ears. How your melodies move has a dramatic effect on the overall sound of your work.

Composers exist who have an unbelievable ability to pull melodies from the air. These composers likely aren't thinking about voice leading when composing because they internalize music in a very intuitive and natural way. Even with a great talent for composition, there is still a need to study composition in a formal way to learn the mechanics of instrumentation, the physics of the orchestra, the proper way to write for performers, and other musical concepts. Even the greatest composers find that studying music composition is necessary to achieve the goal of creating interesting musical works.

When we talk about voice leading, we are referring to the shape and movement of a melody. Many principles of voice leading deal with music from the sixteenth and eighteenth centuries. For this text, I have removed any voice leading rules that aren't useful or relevant to modern composers. For a complete course in voice leading, it's recommended you pick up a book dedicated to contrapuntal practices. Johann Joseph Fux is a theorist who wrote a great book on counterpoint titled *Gradus ad Parnassum*, which deals with voice leading issues.

Conventional voice leading follows our commonsense understanding of gravity, motion, and balance. Imagine a bouncing ball. Certain imperfections in the ball and the floor are present from the first time you bounce that ball. You might not be aware of these imperfections, but they exist. When you bounce a ball, it reaches a certain height. Consecutive bounces will never go as high as the original bounce. Leaps in music are very much like this. If you leap an octave, traditional voice leading would suggest you resolve that leap in the opposite direction. In this way, we maintain an appropriate mix of expansion and contraction, which tends to result in exciting melodies.

As you think about how music relates to nature, you will begin to understand and see similarities that exist. The principles of voice leading will give you a set of guidelines, which you can use to create active and forward-moving lines. As you gain experience, you will start to learn how and when to break these rules — practicing conventional voice leading will teach you how to create balanced melodies.

It's up to you and your imagination to create captivating melodies. However, by learning voice leading guidelines, you can take advantage of the knowledge gained from the composers who came before you. Follow the guidelines now, so that later, you can break them intelligently.

Many modern composers go out of their way to actively work against the principles of voice leading. While there isn't anything wrong with taking your own path, students should first learn how the composers of the past developed their works. A proper foundation ensures the development of sound technique, and it will also help to create an understanding of why these antiquated voice-leading procedures were part of the common practice for hundreds of years.

Traditional Voice Leading Rules

These are the voice leading rules that help you determine how to organize a melody and create chord progressions based on most tonally centric music. Voice leading guidelines for modern composers are generally not the same.

1. Melodic lines are primarily stepwise; when using a leap, the line generally changes direction immediately after the leap and proceeds stepwise so that the "skipped" tones are filled in, at least partially.
2. No more than four intervals of the same type should appear in a row.
3. Melodies should have one high point and one low point, if possible, but having one low point is less crucial.
4. Avoid parallel and contrary unisons, perfect fifths, and perfect octaves when you have intervals.
5. Use the shortest motion between voices in consecutive chords. The goal is to use primarily stepwise motion in all of your chords.
6. Make sure to resolve any tendency tones.
   - The seventh scale degree of a key should resolve up.
   - Diminished fifth intervals should resolve inward to a third.
   - Augmented fourth intervals should resolve outward to a sixth.
   - The seventh of any seventh chord will typically resolve down since there is a dissonance that has a tendency to want to resolve between the root and the seventh of the chord.

The last guideline occurs most often with V7 chords, where the chordal third and seventh creates a diminished fifth. Additionally, the chordal third of the V7 chord in any key is the leading tone, so it tends to resolve up. There are also exceptions to all of these rules, which are taught in traditional harmony courses.

Modern Voice Leading Rules

In contemporary music, voice leading guidelines are significantly relaxed and often dependent on the individual composer. When you write your melodies, you should still aim to move in the opposite direction of any leaps if you want a theme that is easy to sing and understand. Stepwise motion can make it easier for vocalists to perform your music and create a more memorable melody, but many modern composers don't often follow the convention of moving by step.

1. It's possible to lessen the effect of dissonance if the interval is approached and left by step. Leaping into a dissonant interval will bring attention to the dissonance.
2. Melodies should resolve in the opposite direction of any skips and leaps. Typically, a resolution by step is the best option, but you should use your ears in your compositions. A good reason to ignore this guideline is if you want to create a melody that sounds extremely expansive, exotic, or exhibit a specific effect.
3. There are four types of motion in music: oblique, parallel, similar, and contrary. It's best to mix up the various types of movement in your chords or intervals to create a more exciting progression. Parallel motion is the least active type of movement because it tends to destroy the independence of the melody and supporting lines. Use parallel motion to combine the sounds of multiple instruments without using the same pitches.

Employ these three essential voice leading rules in your compositions, and you'll find many of your compositions can be significantly improved. Voice leading is a much more complicated subject, but this is enough to get you started. Taking a course in counterpoint will help you learn more about voice leading rules and how to resolve tones.

Form

Form provides organization in music and places all of the elements into sections that make the music more understandable to the listener. A good motive often dictates the shape of the form while the rhythm may determine the length. Having the ability to envision the duration of musical works comes only with time and experience. Form provides the container for all musical ideas in the piece.

It's not always apparent to a beginning composer that a short and fast motive often results in a more extended composition, while longer motives often result in the creation of shorter pieces. Very simply, the reason for this is that a more extended motive takes more time to perform. Longer motives require the listener to hold more information in their mind when listening to music, and the tempo also tends to be slower. For the sake of comprehensibility, a more extended motive typically results in a shorter piece. With a quick, fast motive, there is less for the listener to remember, and developments and permutations happen more quickly.

Composers study the traditional forms to get a sense of how and why these forms work. Studying structure provides a pathway to learn from the masters of the past. Once the composer establishes an understanding of the existing forms, the next step involves branching out and creating original forms. The elements of a musical work can come together to develop motives and cornerstones, which also results in the realization of the musical form. Rhythm, articulations, dynamics, and pitch can all have a dramatic impact in defining the characteristics of each section in a musical composition.

Basic Musical Forms

Uppercase letters are typically used to denote the various sections within a form. Some of the most common musical forms include strophic form, through-composed, binary, and ternary form. Remember that motives can help determine the form that will work best for your needs. You may even break apart a motive that spells out a C major triad (C-E-G) so that the first section is in the key of C, the second section moves to E, and the third section ends on G, with a final return to C in the fourth section.

124

Strophic Form: This is a form that is primarily used in vocal music, though with some creativity, you can adapt it to any instrument. In a strophic form, the same melody repeats for each verse. Vocal music can get away with this because the lyrics change even if the music stays the same. You could label this type of form as A, A', A", where each new 'apostrophe' symbol indicates a slightly modified version of the original verse. The piece might use superscript numbers instead of apostrophe symbols.

Through-Composed: In a through-composed piece, there is no repetition of sections. Effectively writing a through-composed work proves difficult since the composition can very quickly lack coherence and is prone to meandering. A typical structure looks like A B C D E F G, and so on.

Binary Form: A two-part structure where each section repeats. It consists of an A section and a B section. The A and B sections should show contrasting ideas, but you can relate these ideas through shared elements. In practice, a simple binary form may use the structure A B. Both the A and B section repeat to sound more like AABB.

Binary form exists in a few formats, including simple binary (simple A and B structure) and rounded binary (brings back a portion the A section at the end of a piece.) Furthermore, a binary form can be broken down into sectional and rounded as well. While binary form is essentially a two-part structure, rounded binary may often look like small ternary when it returns to the A section. Since the A section is only a partial repeat of material, it's still considered binary.

Ternary Form: This is a three-part form that may initially look like a binary form. The main feature of this type of structure is that the main A idea comes back after a contrasting B section. Theorists label the form as ABA with no repeats of the individual parts. Although, a *Da Capo* may be used to indicate that the musician should return to the A section and play until the *Fine,* which would be listed right before the B section. Ternary form is a complex form since there are many forms that share its name, including small ternary and full ternary form. However, a full discussion of these forms must be reserved for a dedicated Form and Analysis text.

In addition to these basic forms, there are also Sonata Form, Theme and Variations, Minuet and Trio, Scherzo and Trio, Rondo, Sonata-Rondo, and other structures that composers should learn. A good book on musical form can go a long way toward helping composers learn how to pour their elements, motives, and smaller cornerstones into the container of form. William E. Caplin has a great text on form titled, *Analyzing Classical Form.*

Harmony (Theory)

Harmony is often created by combining multiple independent lines (counterpoint) to create both chords and melodic-motivic content that supports the melody and provide a sense of progression towards a goal. While harmony is often used to give the impression of movement, it can also halt progress when a chord succession is employed. I've included two basic definitions to help you understand the difference between a chord progression and succession.

Chord Progression: a series of chords that lead to a harmonic goal, such as the tonic-dominant-tonic phrase model found in so many classical and romantic era works.

Chord Succession: a series of chords that don't have a harmonic goal but may or may not be related by common tones, motives, or other musical devices.

In the philosophy of composition discussed in this text, motives play a significant role in the creation of harmony. Historically, music theory stems from the study of counterpoint, but musicians often study it as its own distinct subject. Haydn, Bach, Mozart, Beethoven, Brahms, and other famous composers all studied counterpoint to learn how to compose. Before we had a centralized system of theory, the concepts of counterpoint and voice leading were the best methods available for composers to learn how to produce music.

The study of harmony requires a complete music theory course that goes over the various chords and progressions found in music. Since this text is intended only as an introduction to music composition, music theory is only superficially covered.

Harmony can serve as the basis for the creation of a motive. In the next musical example below, the piece begins on a C major chord with a doubled root. By arpeggiating the notes of the C major chord, you can create a motive from the harmony. The motive is then quickly manipulated and developed.

The slurs show the motives that emerge from the harmony.

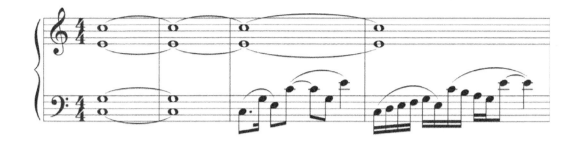

While this is a simple illustrative example that showcases the concept of how harmony can dictate melody, you can imagine how this concept also applies in more sophisticated ways. Maybe you would begin a piece with a cluster chord and then let a motive rise out of that chord. There are numerous possibilities when you start to think about how your motives can be used to create and expand your harmonies.

Orchestration

Orchestration frames the various elements in a way that makes them easier to isolate and identify. In the same way that the color white will stand out on a black background, the choice of instrument combinations can make individual elements stand out. Using contrasting instrument timbres helps the different elements take on specific personalities and characters, which in turn makes the work more memorable to the listener. Instruments bring the element of timbre to bear and help create music that is colorful and interesting.

The concept of orchestration is an entire area of study, much like the other cornerstones. In general, composers should pair instruments in a way that will result in the best sound for a particular musical moment. A good way to learn orchestration is to pick up a book on the topic and find ways to get musical works performed. Hearing your music played is a great way to understand how instruments work together. I once had the opportunity to take a private lesson with Samuel Adler, and he has an excellent book on Orchestration. It's considered one of the most authoritative books available on the market, and I highly suggest you seek it out to learn orchestration. The book is titled *The Study of Orchestration*.

Orchestration helps students learn how to score for strings and write for woodwind, brass, and percussion instruments. It also teaches how to combine instruments in ways that provide the best color and balance in an orchestra. As a composer, you must study orchestration, but you should also understand that when you combine elements with orchestration, you can start to create even more coherence in a piece.

Imagine a woodwind and brass duo that plays a particular motive in a prominent manner within a larger ensemble. Then, the piano comes in and another motive is introduced. After this, the woodwind and brass motive returns, but this time it's in another combination of instruments. The original motive is still recognized, but the meaning of the motive begins to change because of the difference in sound and color.

Elements can help to clarify certain aspects of an orchestration to create better coherence. Imagine a primary motive that begins with a particular instrument section.

Whenever this section comes in, it only plays at a dynamic level of *piano*. Other sections in the ensemble may play at differing dynamic levels, but if the primary motive always uses the same dynamic, the orchestration begins to serve a functional role. Now, imagine that the primary motive changes, but the dynamic level and instrument ensemble stay the same. This creates coherence and the listener now associates the new motive as being related to the primary motive even if it's a dramatically different motive. However, in order to make orchestration serve a functional role, notice that it required the implementation of an element. Orchestration can create cohesion by applying a different motive or melody to each ensemble. If each time the brass section comes in, a particular motive is played, the audience begins to associate that motive with the brass.

Even individual instruments can begin to take on a functional role. Imagine a four-note melody, where each instrument plays a different note of the melody. Perhaps the clarinets play the first note of the melody. The trumpets play the second note. Then, the violin plays the third note. A timpani roll now comes in to play the fourth note.

Now, imagine that each instrument plays the four-note melody again, but this time the melody is expanded. The clarinets play the same first note of the four-note melody followed by a new note that wasn't in the initial four-note melody, which serves to expand the melody. The trumpets play the second note of the four-note motive followed by a new note as well. The violin and the timpani also continue this process. The piece continues until each instrument (or ensemble) is playing a complete motive that combines into an expansive melody that floats around the orchestra. Perhaps at the end, the ensembles break apart and begin to play complete melodies based on their initial motives simultaneously in their own registral space, which the composer was able to implement because of their understanding of counterpoint. (If you decide to use this concept in your own composition, I'll gladly accept a dedication as the inspiration behind your composition.)

By this point, it should begin to become clear how you can combine elements and motives with cornerstones. Since this text is more of an introduction to an idea, it's enough to bring to your attention the fact that orchestration, elements, and motives can work together to create even more cohesion in your composition.

Counterpoint

Counterpoint serves as a precursor to harmony and form. It's a combination of harmony and voice leading since the rules allow a composer to create harmony through voice leading. Counterpoint functions as its own system that can be infused with elements to create dynamic musical works, which make it possible for listeners to hear multiple independent lines that serve a melodic and harmonic function. While I define counterpoint as a cornerstone, it acts as a system of composition in its own right. Counterpoint study teaches students how two or more independent lines combine to create harmony. In many ways, studying counterpoint is more important for a composer than harmony.

For this text, there is no need to separate the closely related cornerstones that work to create counterpoints. Counterpoint plays a role in the construction of a phrase and contributes to the creation of melody and harmony. Counterpoint is made up of several elements, so it makes the most sense to consider it a cornerstone. However, it also dictates how melody and harmony are fused, and it can dictate what kind of form a piece should use based on the guidelines that govern the length of a melody. Counterpoint serves as the glue that holds a composition together.

Since counterpoint relies on a few basic principles, the next few sections will give you a basic overview of contrapuntal practices. I've based the guidelines on sixteenth-century counterpoint, but some flexibility with the rules has been allowed for brevity. One thing you should know is that all counterpoint exercises use the cantus firmus as the basis for the work. The term cantus firmus translates to "fixed voice." Traditionally, the student doesn't change the notes of the cantus firmus, which is provided by the teacher. The counterpoint is the voice written by the student. Many details go into creating a counterpoint, but a complete discussion of sixteenth-century counterpoint would require another book.

Here are a few basic guidelines for species counterpoint according to sixteenth-century guidelines:

- Direct motion (similar or parallel) motion into a perfect consonance is not allowed.

- Musicians considered the fourth a dissonance in the sixteenth century. Composers can use the fourth melodically but not harmonically. So, the fourth could appear in a melody, but not as an interval between the cantus firmus and counterpoint.

- The penultimate note needs to be the leading tone (a half-step away from the final note.) The only exception was that the mode that started on E (called Phrygian) used a whole step between the last two notes. The reason for this is the first and second degree of the mode form a minor second, which many theorists refer to as a descending leading tone. If the seventh scale degree was raised, it would create too much harmonic tension. This 2-1 motion is also the basis for the Phrygian half-cadence that occurs primarily in Baroque music.

First Species

In first species counterpoint, the composer is asked to create a one-on-one relationship of whole notes to whole notes. The composer could use any note values, but traditionally, the composer used whole notes to simplify the process. While a complete explanation is beyond the scope of this text, first species uses a series of consonant intervals to create a composition that removes any dissonance. On a larger scale, most pieces can be reduced to a first species counterpoint example as well. Though, it's challenging to create an exciting composition based on a first species example (a concept that is explained further in the later species.)

(Example from Fux)

For this text, notice how each note in the counterpoint uses consonant intervals, and the piece progresses using primarily stepwise motion. The numbers between the counterpoint and cantus firmus relate to the generic intervals used. A counterpoint that uses stepwise motion principally in the melody and contrary motion between the two voices produces an effective composition.

Second Species

In second species, half notes are added to the counterpoint to allow for dissonance on the offbeat. The rule is that all dissonances must be approached and resolved by step. If you try to complete a second species exercise by using the framework of a first species exercise, you'll run into some underlying issues since all of the species tend to use stepwise motion. The stepwise motion of first species makes it difficult to add dissonance in between the tones.

Notice that in measure 5–6, the notes of the counterpoint changed from the first species example. The original first species counterpoint moved from B to C. In this second species version, the dissonant passing tone results in a move on the downbeats from B up to D. Skipping up to D on the offbeat of measure 5 would have resulted in parallel fifths moving down to the C of the first species exercise in measure 6. While a leap could be used to keep the original B and C in measures 5 and 6 of the first species exercise, this would result in a more disjunct counterpoint, and the goal is to use as much stepwise motion as possible with only a few skips or leaps. Depending on the composer teaching you counterpoint, the skips in measures 3-4 may not be allowed. Measure 2-3 may also prove problematic since there is a skip followed by a leap.

(Example modified from Fux First Species)

The example for second species serves as an attempt to use the original first species notes, but you'll see that it doesn't match up well as the counterpoint continues. The only way to ensure a reduction to first species requires beginning with a more complex species and then reducing it to first species. However, moving in stepwise motion would result in either a poor first or second species example; this makes it very difficult to start with first species and then modify the original first species example to create the other species. First species is intended to serve as a starting point to learn about consonance and dissonance, as well as basic voice leading rules.

Third Species

Third species uses four quarter notes against each half note. Dissonance is allowed between the consonant notes, and you'll notice that the first and third beat of each measure also features a consonance. There are some exceptions where dissonance appears on beats two and four with the addition of specific off-beat patterns such as the cambiata and double neighbor tones. Additionally, dissonance could occur on the second, third, or fourth beat, provided the dissonance passes between two consonant notes. The important thing to note is that the counterpoint uses four notes to every one note of the cantus firmus.

(Example from Fux)

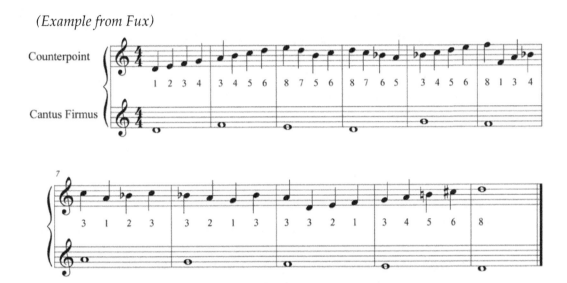

135

Fourth Species

Fourth species is a technique of suspensions. In this species, the composer begins to learn how to use suspensions as an embellishment to make a counterpoint example more exciting and to effectively allow dissonances on the downbeats. Notice that this example shows primarily 7-6 suspensions. The 4-3 suspension provides another option. Some texts allow the 2-1 suspension because the unison occurs on an offbeat, which is the only permitted placement for a unison.

Additionally, when the cantus firmus appears above the counterpoint, a 2-3 suspension is allowed beneath. The numbers in the suspension indicate the generic interval from the lowest note between the two lines.

(Example from Fux)

Composers treated dissonance in music carefully, but a small amount of dissonance on weak beats was deemed desirable. Placing the dissonance on a soft beat allowed it to sneak by the consonance and not bring too much attention to itself. Dissonances that resolved to a consonance propelled the piece forward. Resolved dissonance creates interest since we have a desire to resolve the tones and expect a resolution.

Fifth Species

Fifth species deals with the combination of all of the species. Fux provides an example based on the same cantus firmus we have been using for the previous four species of counterpoint. Notice that in fifth species, there are also some eighth notes added for interest. These embellishments of the suspension were typical, and composers learned to ornament their species counterpoints before moving on to third species.

(Example from Fux)

Notice that if you tried to reduce a fifth species counterpoint to a first species counterpoint, a lot of leaps and skips between the downbeats would occur.

An initial ascent to the top of the counterpoint is common in classical music. The F located in the seventh measure quickly resolves using a basic stepwise pattern to the first scale degree in the final measure. This 3-2-1 scale degree motion often appears in classical music, and it's often considered a characteristic of classical music compositions.

The notes between scale degrees 3-2-1 can be viewed as embellishments of a basic melodic line. Schenkerian analysis uses this type of structuring.

Counterpoint Goals

The goal of counterpoint was to serve as an instructional method to teach composers how to compose music. The student started with simple exercises. After attaining mastery, they moved on to more complex tasks. Eventually, composers combined the four species to create a fifth species of free counterpoint that employed concepts from each species. The concepts included consonance on downbeats from the first species, dissonance on the offbeat from second species, stepwise melodic motion with passing, neighbor and other types of embellishments from third species, and dissonance on the downbeat with fourth species. Additionally, some new ornamentations are allowed to make the fifth species more interesting.

The concept of counterpoint, like all of the other cornerstones, is deep and complex. One way to learn counterpoint is to pick up *Gradus ad Parnassum* by Joseph Fux. It's a short read with plenty of examples to help students along. The text also discusses the most common problems. One minor flaw in the text occurs when Fux leaves it up to the student to use a concept known as the battuta. A battuta occurs when an interval of a tenth moves by contrary (stepwise) motion into an octave. The battuta never appeared in two-part sixteenth-century counterpoint, so it's generally best to avoid using this feature. It tends to make the piece sound like it comes to a cadence wherever it appears. Cadences end the motion of the melody, so it's best to avoid the battuta in music.

Motives

Motives have an essential role in building the melody, impacting the harmony, and influencing the various cornerstones employed by a composer. Motives serve as the building blocks of any composition.

Densely packed motives may contain every possible element available in music, but this is also not a requirement of a motive and dense motives aren't very flexible. Compact motives tend to result in concise and brief works.

Motives don't fit neatly into the elements camp or the cornerstone camp because they contain components of each and can impersonate the role of an element or a cornerstone depending on their usage. For this reason, the motive serves a critical role in music composition. Motives act as a bridge between elements and cornerstones.

Understanding the function and purpose of a motive is a vital part of being a composer. Motives create phrases, aid in development, support and instigate modulations, and play a fundamental role in the progression of a piece. The motive can also affect the creation of harmony in composition. Motives are small but essential to the success of a musical work.

So, what is the motive? It's the basic building block of music, and it plays a part in many aspects of the development of a composition. Motives are considered the smallest complete musical ideas, but just because they are complete doesn't mean they can stand on their own.

Music does exist that is not reliant on a motive. This type of music is rare and often hard to follow. It uses a process generically referred to as musical gesturing. A gesture could be as uncomplicated as the imitation of movement or the contour of a rising and falling melody. A gesture is simply a term used to describe more specific changes to a set of motives, such as augmentation, retrograde movement, isomelos, and other techniques designed to catalyze variations in a musical work. Several specific gestures exist that composers can use, and they fall under the umbrella of "variation" in most music theory texts since gestures play a large role in the creation of musical works that use the theme and variation form.

Motive Reorganization

You can create more than one melody out of a single melody by combining various motives from each theme into one new melody. As an example, we'll use two melodies from Mozart's Sonata No. 15.

Both of the melodies are relatively simple melodies, but they don't share too much in common. However, these two melodies can combine into a new melody that bears the likeness of both melodies. In many ways, this is similar to when parents have a child that takes on characteristics of both parents. It's possible to identify the features of each parent and how they transferred to the child. If humans can find comparisons with something as organic and subtle as a child's features, it makes sense that it's also possible to do this with melodies. Play these melodies on an instrument if you can't hear them internally.

Melody A

Melody B

A third melody can be created using these two melodies as the basis. In the example for Melody C, I've used parts of the motives from the first melody with pieces from the second. Notice how elements from the first and second melody fuse in a way that creates a third melody.

Melody C - Combination of Melody A and B

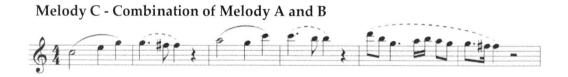

The solid slur shows the motives from Melody A. The dashed slur shows the motives from Melody B.

140

At this point, there are two things I'd like you to notice about Melody C:

- Combining two motives helps to integrate the original two melodies more deeply into the composition.
- Integrating motives from both melodies gives the piece better cohesion since the motivic elements from both melodies create the third melody of the work.

Notice how in measures 2 and 4, the pitches are transposed while the interval relationship was maintained. Transposition is one of the most common methods used to develop a motive.

Melody C is somewhat stilted to illustrate a rough draft skeleton that demonstrates clearly how motives can be combined. We assume the composer would continue to work out this melody to find a way to make it flow as effortlessly as the original melodies, but that might require more development and obscure the relationship to melodies A and B. The art of music composition comes in when you refine the new melody, keep aspects of the original melodies, and create something new.

While this new melody contains motives from Melody A and B, notice how it is not using any dynamics or articulations. Adding additional elements would help tie these two motives together even more. In the actual composition, Mozart spends quite a bit of time preparing for the introduction of Melody B. If he continued the composition toward our new Melody C, he would likely prepare the introduction of this melody by breaking apart (fragmenting) the various motives to prepare us for the reconstruction that is to come later.

When using three melodies in close proximity, the risk of making the piece ramble becomes an issue. There is also a fine line between too much and too little motivic development in a piece. As a general rule, you'll want to keep one or two melodies per section. If the piece is long, returning to the melodies from the initial section can help tie everything together. Of course, keeping only one or two melodies per section is meant only as a general guide, and it is not a rule of composition.

Mozart uses a simple sequence to prepare for the introduction of his second melody. Using a repeated scale and rhythmic pattern that recurs on various scale degrees, he can prepare for the key change and introduce the second melody. Notice how the sequences based on the initial motive in the second measure prepare and develop the initial motive to bring about the new melody in measure 13 of the example. He also prepares for the new melody by throwing in some accidentals in measure 9 as the melody moves from C major to D major.

Depending on your theory background, you may analyze this as a tonicization or a modulation. However, recognize how Mozart uses accidentals to bring about the new melody with a different tonic pitch class, which is a fancy way of saying that Mozart has moved from C as the tonal basis for the melody to D. Essentially, Mozart is preparing us for the key change coming up. The motive he used as a transition begins as a dotted quarter to sixteenth-note figure in measure 2. To make the development of one of the motives in Mozart's piece more apparent, I've used a dashed slur. Notice how the motive changes but maintains some of the initial rhythmic element.

Motives don't have to be limited to melodic notes that move "horizontally." Harmonic "vertical" motives also exist, but for those to be effective, the harmonic idea must be recognizable. In Wagner's *Tristan und Isolde*, there is a long extended English horn solo. At the end of the solo is a chord known as the "Tristan" chord:

Theorists have attempted to analyze the chord with little consensus. This chord is easily discernable as a half-diminished seventh chord, and it stands out from the rest of the piece, partially due to its presentation – the chord is extended and prolonged. Because of the extension, the motive that precedes it and comes immediately after and during the chord becomes more noticeable and helps draw the listener's attention to a critical thematic element in the piece. What's unusual about the chord is how it's resolved in relation to the surrounding harmony. This chord is primarily made up of an augmented fourth, augmented sixth, and augmented ninth above the bass note. The chord could be analyzed as a French augmented sixth chord, a modified pre-dominant, or even a secondary dominant with a lowered fifth.

While I'm sure you're itching to discover an explanation for the chord, the truth is that no theorists can agree on a single analysis. The primary purpose of this book is to give you examples of how you can compose your own music and create your own riddles for theorists to solve. However, let's take one possible analysis of what is happening here using the concepts of elements, motives, and cornerstones.

The same chord also appears in Beethoven's Sonata, Op. 31, No. 3. However, Beethoven writes the chord within the key while Wagner's "Tristan" uses accidentals that indicate a chromatic movement. In the example above, the Tristan chord resolves eventually to a dominant seventh chord with the E, G#, B, and D in the measure following its introduction. While you could reasonably analyze the harmony using any of these explanations, it makes sense to see this as a progression to the dominant of A minor. Wagner arrives at A minor through simple chromatic voice leading. For our purposes, the motive is simply a chromatic motion.

Let's take this apart further so that the explanation is more precise. Whether theorists accept the analysis that ensures is less important than the composition lesson that it provides. Let's isolate the melody and break it down into a smaller motive. You can see that there is essentially a very easy to recognize two-note motive.

1. In the first measure, the motive uses a dotted quarter note tied to a quarter note. This elemental rhythm is then expanded by the element of pitch, using a simple half step relationship.
2. The motive is repeated and developed a whole step higher on the G# downbeat moving up a half step to A at the end of the measure. This is an inversion of the original descending half-step motive.
3. At the end of the chromatic progression, the rhythmic continues and the pitch motive stays the same with a whole step leading from the G# on the downbeat of measure 2 to an A# on the downbeat of measure 3.

So, what about the bass notes? It does appear that the goal is the fifth scale degree of A minor, which would be E. Functionally, this makes sense through the lens of tonal harmony, where the I chord (the tonic) often moves toward the V chord (the dominant).

The first thing to notice is how the lowest voice (bass) and the upper-middle voice (alto) moves down by a half step, which mimics the half step descent of the first measure and second measure. Contrapuntally, this makes sense because it allows the

144

bottom and upper voices to move in the opposite (contrary) motion. Contrary motion is considered a desirable motion since it lends more independence to the musical line than direct or oblique motion.

Now, notice the voice exchange between the lower inner voice (tenor) and the highest voice (soprano.) A voice exchange is a well-documented concept in music theory, where the voices between two chords switch places in different octaves. In this case, the B3 of the first chord in the tenor in third measure "exchanges" with the B4 of the soprano in the fourth measure. The G#4 of the soprano in measure 3 "exchanges" with the G#3 of the tenor in measure 4.

The final thing to point out is how the entire melody moves out of the harmonic framework present in the second measure. That F to B tritone relationship in the bass clef serves as a framework for the entire melody that ascends from F to B. Notice how harmony, counterpoint, motive, pitch, and rhythm come together to create cohesion from the opening of the solo F to the final resting point on B?

As if this wasn't enough, Wagner even takes this one step further, which is shown by the analysis below:

- The A3, which is the tonic of the key, is repeated at the octave right before the arrival on V in the third measure.

- The F4 is continued contrapuntally an octave lower from the second measure in the treble to the third measure in the bass.
- The E4 at the end of the second measure repeats in the bass of the fourth measure, following the initial half step motive relationship in the second measure. This is repeated again with the G#4 in the treble falling down to the G#3 in the bass.
- Finally, note the position of the bass F-B tritone interval. It sits squarely in the middle of the phrase serving as the harmonic framework in which the F-B melodic motive emerges. In this sense, harmony and motive build off each other.

Take note of the way the F4 in the second measure moves in half steps past the E4 to the D#4 and arrives at the D4. This half step motion is contrapuntally using contrary motion against the whole step movement from F– G#–A–B. You may also note how the E in the second measure jumps up a major third to the G# in the third measure, which helps to create coherence for the major third interval sitting in the bass of the fourth measure.

With so many possible ways to see how the fundamental elements of the motive are developed and expanded in a contrapuntal, harmonic, rhythmic, and elemental way, it's hard to deny that Wagner wasn't at least aware of these relationships when writing this composition. Ultimately, I'm not trying to prove an analysis of the Tristan chord. Instead, I'm trying to demonstrate how the elements and cornerstones work together to create coherence in a piece. Whether or not a theorist would accept these relationships is another matter entirely. The critical thing to note is that there is a recognizable pattern in these few measures, and you can find these patterns on the micro and the macro level of most compositions if you know how to look for them.

Still not convinced? Then, take a look at how Beethoven uses the same chord in his Piano Sonata No. 18. This chord is also found in works by Guillaume de Machaut, Carlo Gesualdo, Bach, Mozart, Chopin, and others. They all use similar motivic developments to arrive at this slightly dissonant sounding chord.

Look at the motive in the first measure moving from Cb to F. It's later revealed harmonically in the bass in the last measure. Beethoven approaches the final chord by moving mostly in half steps. From the F in the bass and the Ab in the soprano, he holds the common tone Cb and the tonic pedal on Eb. (A tonic pedal doesn't have to occur in the bass).

Additionally, the inner bass voices sound out that F to Ab relationship that is later revealed in the melody moving from measure three to four. As with Wagner, there is much more to the elemental development that builds the motive bridge that leads to the phrase cornerstone. Still, you should understand by now how you can hide the various elements to make elements, motives, and cornerstones work together for cohesion.

While this little foray into Wagner and Beethoven is fascinating, it's more important to understand what it has to do with editing and creating your motives. The motive has to be memorable for it to be effective. Wagner creates a great motive by introducing a highly unusual chord, but he doesn't just introduce the chord. He sits upon the chord for a rather extended duration while reiterating the rhythm presented in the previous measure.

The emphasis on rhythm accomplishes two things: *it creates an impression that the rhythm is essential*, and *it establishes foreshadowing in the piece*. Wagner uses the rhythm later on in the composition for additional dramatic effect.

One of the interesting features of this chord is that it consists of two sets of dissonances, in which only one of the dissonances gets resolved. Wagner created a highly recognizable motive by introducing it memorably. Beethoven did the same thing by leaping from the top and bottom notes of his goal harmony. Your motives should also be memorable, so you should aim to do something remarkable with each motive you create.

Motivic Elements

A motive should consist of only a few notes, be catchy, and easy to remember. Most music that we remember and grow attached to has a sense of logic, form, and a certain degree of complexity to make it possible for the listener to hear new elements with each further listening.

Even free-flowing American Indian music has a repetitive nature that creates a structure. Structure helps a listener to remember the essential elements in a composition. Firmly establishing the home key reveals one of the reasons for the classical period's literal repeat of a sonata exposition. The repeat helps to ingrain the most critical elements in the listener's mind. After all, they did not have recordings back then that allowed the audience to listen to a piece several times. Composers had to use repetition to help the listener gain familiarity. We still hear this sort of repetition today in rock and popular music.

Concert music tends to take more time to get from one section to another. Mainstream music takes less time to get from point A to B. Repeating the exposition in concert music ensured that the listener had time to grasp and become comfortable with the primary material before further development.

Understanding the rationale and function of a motive is an essential part of being a composer. The motive helps to build phrases, allows for manipulations and modulations, and it has a fundamental impact on the progression of a piece. It is the basic building block of music and plays a part in many aspects of a composition.

Tom Zatar Kay is an artist that throws paint against a canvas. The art lies in the various actions that he utilizes when creating a work of art. A strong thrust will create one impression on the canvas while a flick of the fingers produces another, and this provides one point of view in art. My sentiment is that he records a memory of that moment in his life. By examining one of his paintings, you can envision the motions that he used. In this way, the audience can imagine a timeline of his activity. Through analysis of the layers of paint, the observer may establish what the very first stroke without ever knowing for certain. With more attention, patterns begin to emerge, and the viewer becomes engaged in the work.

Some critics argue against his methods, but he creates art in a way that resonates with his style and ideas. Art that lacks a unique voice, style, and conviction often ends up being derivative of another artists' work.

Zatar has the benefit of letting the audience unravel his art over time since most artwork is static. Music functions as a time art, and the listener doesn't get to listen to a composition at a tempo that allows for deep contemplation of every chord. Because of this, composers typically must use some form of repetition to help the listener along. Using too little repetition leaves the listener feeling lost while too much will be boring. A balance must exist to keep the composition interesting while still providing an incentive to listen to the entire work. Not all art has to be immediately identifiable and beautiful to behold. Sometimes the beauty of something only comes with time.

Motives can be as simple as the three-note motive from the Bach Brandenburg Concerto. The motive develops at several pitch levels, and it ends up creating compound melody with each melody maintaining its independence by placing it in its own registral space. In the example below, the G-F#-G is repeated and serves as one melody. There is then a sort of unfolding where the melody jumps down to a similar D-C-D motive. The entire line is stabilized since the G-F#-G motive continues to recur and serves as the tonic grounding force of the piece.

When you're writing your motives, it makes sense to write whatever comes to mind. Once you have written your motives down, you can begin to edit them so that they can be used to create cohesiveness in your musical work. Consider the following questions:

1. Is my motive memorable?
2. Does it create the mood I'm trying to convey?
3. Does it sound like it belongs in the piece, and is it related to the melody?
4. Is it too complex or too simple to be recognizable as a complete thought?

5. How many elements does it consist of, and can I reduce any of the elements to serve a functional role that will be recognizable later in the piece? Or do the elements serve a primarily non-functional role that the listener would not be able to identify later in the piece?

By getting into the habit of thinking about how you can use your motives in various ways, you will start to get a wealth of ideas, and your compositions will begin to flourish. Using the elements non-functionally is perfectly fine, but you should have enough elements that serve a functional role to allow you to continue developing your piece with functional coherence.

Combining Components

Elements, motives, and cornerstones work together. In most cases, you can't have a motive without at least two elements. Likewise, you can't have a cornerstone without motives and elements. Dynamics, articulation, tempo, rhythm, and other elements combine to make motives. The motives are then used to create phrases. In some instances, they create the form for the entire piece. When a composition includes several similar elements within each motive and cornerstone, a piece begins to become coherent. Elements give a composition definition and cornerstones give a composition shape. The more elements that are repeated within a motive or cornerstone, the more coherence a piece tends to have.

Throughout the text, examples have been provided to give you an idea of how to combine components. However, now that the components of music have been discussed, it's possible to review previous concepts to reinforce concepts of coherence. Essentially, elements are building blocks that can be joined together into motives to create the more significant cornerstones of a musical composition and to relate cornerstones to the piece as a whole. If a composer keeps the elements in mind throughout the creation of a work, then it's possible to create a personal and expressive work that develops in a logical way.

When a composer creates a motive using just pitch and rhythm, the motive can then be modified and infused with the other elements. Dynamics, articulations, and even specific instruments can be combined to create coherence and comprehensibility within a musical work. Motives end up serving a functional role to connect different sections in the composition, and unlike elements, a motive rarely serves a purely decorative purpose.

Phrases typically consist of smaller motives since motives serve to create the phrase and develop the musical work. Those motives may have a dynamic marking of *piano* and use a highly recognizable rhythm that helps to make the motive more memorable to the listener. The rhythm might then be combined with other elements by changing the articulation or tempo to build and develop the composition. If these elements of articulation and tempo are used in a functional and highly visible way, then the elements can be isolated to create coherence later on in the musical work.

In the Orchestration section of the text, the concept of using dynamics to create coherence was introduced. Diving deeper into this concept, imagine the majority of a piece is played at a *forte* dynamic level, but there is a two-bar motive that is played at *piano* every time it occurs, and this is the only time the piece drops down to a *piano* marking. The defining elements of this motive are dynamic markings and the two-measure length, so I'll refer to it as the *piano* motive. You could use any label as long as the concept is clearly understood.

The marked difference in dynamic level will make the *piano* motive stand out. If it is used later in the piece, but it still occurs for about two measures and is played at *piano*, the audience should be able to relate it to the original *piano* motive. Here, two elements combine (dynamics and measures) to make it possible to create a modification of the motive that still relates to the larger motivic development goals in the composition.

Using dynamics functionally can be tricky because the dynamic element has to stand out by itself for it to be memorable. In the *piano* motive example, the dynamic stands out because the piece is mostly played at a loud dynamic level, so when the rare occurrence happens where the piece suddenly gets quiet, the audience notices and relates it to other circumstances that use the same dynamic level. The advantage of pulling this type of coherence off is that the *piano* motive can change in any number of ways to create a piece that develops in a wild and often unpredictable way. In this instance, perhaps the new version of the *piano* motive begins initially with a two-bar motive at a piano marking, and then suddenly expands and contorts at a frenetic and loud *forte* dynamic marking before finally coming back down to another *piano* marking to create the next section.

If you're following the logic, you can begin to see how an element can serve a few purposes. In all of the scenarios below, assume that the elements of dynamic and measure stays the same, but other elements such as pitch and rhythm are not defined. This means that the pitch and rhythm could change, but the *piano* motive will still be recognized as belonging to the original idea.

1. The *piano* motive creates coherence by using dynamics to connect motives that have the potential to be otherwise unrelated. *This is an example of an element aiding in the development of a motive.*
2. The *piano* motive also has the potential to create form, with the *piano* marking serving as a divider between different formal ideas. *This is an example of an element aiding in defining the borders of a form.*
3. The piano motive can be used to both develop a motive and create form. *This is an example of how the piano motive can be infused within a musical work and function as an element, motive, or cornerstone.*

In the first two examples, the motive helps to create coherence in a composition. Only the third example begins the process of creating an *organic composition* because of its infusion into every aspect of the composition, which is discuss in more detail in Part IV.

A motive can be created using a combination of any two elements, but this isn't as straightforward as it may seem. If you try to create a motive that uses only the elements of pitch and articulation, then you will find that you likely also need a rhythm. Rhythms can change if they are not essential to the motive, but it is very difficult to create a melody without some sense of rhythm. A melody without rhythms would likely involve the combination of pitches at unrelated rhythmic intervals without a pulse or beat. This contrasts with a melody that has a rhythm that changes erratically, but the elements of pitch and articulation remain consistent. Put another way, instead of the rhythm staying the same each time a motive is repeated, it may vary widely while still using the same sequence of pitches and articulations. Because the motive maintains pitch and articulation, it will always be relatable to the original motive even if the rhythm bears no resemblance to the original motive's rhythm.

By combining pitch and rhythm in various ways, you can create several different phrases that all sound related to each other because they share the same elements. Now, let's say you add a dynamic to those motives. Now, the piece is even more coherent because dynamics are being used in addition to pitch and rhythm to create your phrases. Add some more elements like articulation and tempo, and you begin to form coherent melodies that relate to each other on several different levels.

Use these elements in combination with the phrase cornerstone to develop the form cornerstone of a composition. In the second section of a work, if you wanted to create a development section, you could look at all of the elements in the first section and isolate them. Maybe you take just the pitch and articulation elements and use a different rhythm to create a new phrase. When you start to think of elements as the building blocks and cornerstones for the container that your piece fits within, you can begin to get extremely creative with your musical ideas while maintaining a high level of coherence.

Composers who understand how elements can be used to build a piece and create coherence realize elements can be used in combination with cornerstones to help tie otherwise unrelated sections of the music together. If the rhythm used in the first motive is repeated later in the composition with completely new pitches to create a new motive, there is still a link between that rhythm and the primary motive. The listener will be able to make a connection between the first motive and the new motive because of the identifiable rhythm. When other elements are also included, this makes the relationship between the two motives even stronger. Add yet another element, such as the particular instruments used in the initial motive, and you'll have a positive relationship between the two motives.

The more elements that are duplicated in the creation of a new idea, the more the two ideas will cohere to each other and sound related. Exact duplication is the most common method of creating coherence, but it's also the least exciting method. Thinking about a melody in terms of its smaller elemental parts can make it possible to create a composition that develops into a large and powerful piece that captures the imagination of the audience.

Plenty of other composers and theorists have pointed out the relationship between the smaller elements of a work and their larger construction. Jean Molino notes that "any element belonging to the total musical fact can be isolated or taken as a strategic variable of musical production." Virgil Thomson notes that rhythm, melody, harmony, counterpoint, and orchestration are all raw materials used to build a composition. While harmony, melody, counterpoint, and orchestration are considered cornerstones in this text, it's conceivable that a broader definition of the elements of music could label these components as elements. Therefore, a description of these concepts is so crucial to the understanding of this text. It's vital to avoid any confusion about what constitutes an element and cornerstone for the purpose of this text.

It should be clear that a motive typically needs to include at least pitch or rhythm as one of the elements. However, even this is not really true. There are ways around using pitch and rhythm as we understand these elements in a musical work, but to think about these elements in a new way, you'll have to get creative. Review the following two examples to get an idea for the possible options:

- Instrument timbre and dynamics could be used together. A foghorn (yes, a foghorn) that plays at a *forte* dynamic level will be recognizable each time it presents itself in a piece.
- Articulation and tempo can also be used without a defined pitch or rhythm. Perhaps a performer is instructed to stomp their foot onto the stage with great force at a *forte* level, and to start slow and gradually pick-up speed without worrying about using a particular rhythm. At another point, the performer might be asked to tap quickly but quietly.

Elements can be combined in any number of combinations, which is why this method of composing is so flexible. When you begin to think about the elements at your disposal, you start to think of composing music in a much more flexible manner. If you're a tonal composer, you can use an organic approach to create your music. If you write atonal music, you can use this approach to compose your music. If you write futurism (it's a thing), you can use this approach to write your music. If you bang on trash cans, this approach also works. It doesn't matter if you're into expressionism, primitivism, futurism, exoticism, symbolism, neoclassism, or any other -ism, you can use this system to make sense of your music.

Learn to think broadly about concepts and you will be able to create musical works that do not define success solely through counterpoint, harmony, phrase, and form. Instead, you will begin to judge your creations based on the concept of coherence and whether or not it functions organically.

PART IV: COMPOSING ORGANICALLY
A SUMMARY OF ORGANIC MUSIC

Music can be written in many different ways, but a piece that functions organically uses elements to build the motives and cornerstones in coherent ways. Infusing elements into both motives and cornerstones can result in music that stands the test of time, doesn't get old, and in fact, gets richer with age.

The following is a quote from Luciano Berio from a collection of interviews with Rossana Dalmonte and Bálint András Varga:

I think that all ways of making, listening to and even talking about music are right in their way. When music has sufficient complexity and semantic depth, it can be approached and understood in different ways. Most commercial songs, and for that matter the sonic wallpaper and the musical tombolas of the self-styled avant-garde, can only be listened to on one level: but there's also music that can be heard on many levels, and is continually generating musical meaning.

The more simple and one-dimensional a musical discourse is, the more diffuse and immediate its relationship to everyday reality.

The more concentrated and complex it is, the more complex and selective are its social relations, and the more ramified its meanings.

So that a song can express of a moment of human work and emotion, and it is an immediately "useful" instrument to people at different times of the day or year: but you can replace one with another. Whereas complex music works are irreplaceable moments in a historical process.

Sometimes I have a strange feeling that musical processes can be more intelligent than the people who produce and listen to them–that the cells of those processes, like the chromosomes of a genetic code, can be more intelligent than the perceptive organs that should be making sense of them. It's as if music were miming one of the most incredible of natural processes: the passage from inanimate to animate life, from molecular to organic forms, from an abstract and immobile dimension to a vital and expressive one.

Music must be capable of educating people to discover and create relations between different elements, and in doing that it speaks to the history of man and of his musical resources in all their acoustic, and expressive, aspects.

Before we continue, I'm going to stress that this part is partially a review of the concepts addressed in this text to help consolidate important concepts. However, I'm reviewing these concepts in a severely condensed summary form with some additional insight into the process of composing music organically.

The aim of this textbook was to introduce the idea of composing organic music so that you can continue your study in music with more knowledge and insight into the process of composing. This section also dives deeper into the concept of coherence and comprehensibility. After reading the text, this section can be used as a summary to refresh concepts in an expedient manner.

Organic Music

Organic – Intrinsic, forming a fundamental and inherent part of something and mostly responsible for its identity or makeup. Occurring or developing gradually and naturally, without being forced or contrived.

An organic work is a work where the elements in a composition function in a cohesive manner to build motives and reinforce the cornerstones of music composition. The goal of creating organic music is to create a coherent, musical, engaging, and understandable work.

Organic music has nothing to do with using sustainably harvested notes or writing on parchment that is made using chemical-free processes. It also doesn't have anything to do with the style of music. In some circles, organic music might refer to the process of using acoustic instruments instead of digital replicas, but that's not how this book uses the term.

"The work of art, like every living thing is conceived as a whole."
~Arnold Schoenberg

Organic music is not a concept found in most music theory textbooks. Still, many composers agree that a musical work can function organically even if a standard definition of the term organic is not defined. Composers tend to intuitively know about the concept of writing organically, but there isn't a guidebook that attempts to explain how to accomplish the task. As with many studies in the more abstract art of composition, students are often expected to reconcile extended concepts on their own or through guidance in music composition lessons. However, most composers tend to teach abstractly and provide suggestions for development rather than focusing on combining disparate elements to create a coherent musical work.

If you've made it this far, then you know that the elements and motives of music create the overarching cornerstones of a work. Essentially, the process of using elements to develop motives and cornerstones is what I refer to as organic music. The practice of using organic composition techniques to teach students serves as an effective and established method for training a composer. However, it is also important to stress that it is not the only way. It is merely the most commonly used method to teach in the beginning stages, and it produces good results since students can quickly see how various aspects of a composition can relate to each other and grow over time. Since music is essentially a time art, it makes sense to compare composing to the process of growth in nature.

The term organic refers to a composition where every element of the composition has a functional role. By now, it should be clear how functional elements, motives, and cornerstones work since it serves as the theme of this entire book. Remember, not every element must be present in every cornerstone to instill a sense of coherence; however, several memorable elements are essential to ensure that each cornerstone builds the composition coherently in a natural and interconnected and organic way.

An understanding of how to write music organically provides composers the tools to compose works based on sound compositional principles, which is essentially an aesthetics of music. An aesthetic of music can be used to produce a variety of music, in the present and future, or to analyze past works. Instead of creating works based on systems designed to remove many of the choices available as a composer, there is no limit to what a composer can create when thinking about how the individual parts relate to the whole. A well-developed aesthetic gives a composer good taste, which can be used to assess a musical work.

Musical Coherence and Comprehensibility

The aim of coherence can be nothing other than comprehensibility:

Something is comprehensible if the whole...consists of parts that have relationships not too remote from each other and from the whole...and if the arrangement of these parts is such that their relationship to each other and the whole is not lost.

~Arnold Schoenberg

The concept of coherence and comprehensibility in music grows out of the unfinished theoretical works of Arnold Schoenberg. Familiarity in a musical work is achieved by creating independent elements that possess features that are also present in other elements of the work and within the larger cornerstones. This is where the elements of a composition combine with motives and the broader cornerstones of a musical work to form a composition where all of the content is related down to the smallest aspects of the work.

Schoenberg supports the concept of organic musical works in which all parts have some essential relationship to other aspects of the composition. The truly beautiful thing about writing music organically is that it doesn't require the composer to change their style of writing. A composer who writes atonal music can compose organically just as easily as someone who models their music after Bach, Beethoven, or Brahms. An organic work includes elements that cohere to each other to form larger cornerstones and that are comprehensible to the listener.

Coherence can be achieved by pairing multiple elements in a music composition to create motives and larger cornerstone structures. Motives that contain elements are then inserted into cornerstones throughout the piece. In some cases, a single element can help to clarify the form or bring out a single motivic idea. The more elements included in a motive, melody, harmony, orchestration, counterpoint, and form, the more coherence there will be in a musical work. Elements must combine to create cornerstones in such a way that the elements retain enough of the original structure to remain recognizable. The elements must not begin to deconstruct too much and lose their shape, structure, and identifiability.

Two ideas cohere if one of them contains a part of the other. Coherence can be so complex that it becomes lost on most listeners, but that doesn't mean that coherence doesn't exist.

Comprehensibility requires a degree of coherence. When a piece includes elements in such a way that motives infuse cornerstones, the piece nears a sense of comprehensibility. For a piece to be comprehensible, the musical elements must make sense. It's not enough to simply insert elements into motives or cornerstones. When a piece uses good voice leading and creates interesting melodic and harmonic lines, the piece gets closer to becoming comprehensible. For a truly comprehensible work, a musician must apply intuition and the tenets of music composition to create a logical work.

When a piece is performed, there is a limited amount of time for the listener to grasp the melodic materials. A piece that uses basic coherence, with simple and easy to recognize parts, will apply to a large audience and be highly comprehensible. A musical work that uses complex coherence and difficult to hear relationships in a work is said to be less comprehensible.

Coherence and comprehensibility require repetition so the listener can pick up on how the composition develops. If there isn't enough repetition, the listener will become lost and unable to follow the piece. When there is too much repetition, the listener loses interest as the piece becomes overly predictable.

One way to make a piece coherent and comprehensible is by using a good motive that is made up of more than one repeating element. Composers should spend more time on motives than any other single aspect of a composition. When creating motives, concentrate on whether the elements play a functional or non-functional role. Motives that play a functional role produce a composition that is highly coherent and comprehensible.

Organizing a Musical Composition

Advanced composers may not think about elements, motives, and cornerstones during the initial creation of a work. Personally, when I'm composing, I let my mind wander, and I only develop an idea when something catches my interest. It's only in the final stages that I begin to analyze my intuitive compositions and edit them for coherence and comprehensibility. I believe this editing process can make the difference between a good and great composition.

Elements of a composition include the pitches, rhythms, dynamics, articulations, and timbre, but this definition can be adapted and edited to suit the needs and beliefs of the individual composer. For example, some composers may decide to make timbre a cornerstone since timbre typically forms from multiple elements. As you know, elements are combined to create what could be considered a third component of music – the motive. The definition of an element is ultimately up to the composer, but this text discussed some of the traditional elements.

Cornerstones are the largest parts of the composition, including melody, form, harmony (theory), counterpoint, and orchestration. Composers can think about additional components that might be classified as a cornerstone and add to this list. I believe the cornerstones I have listed are the most important cornerstones to make a piece comprehensive, but there may be more or less depending on the style of music.

These definitions may change depending on the goals desired, but they can serve as a starting point for conceptualizing organic music.

Regardless of how components are organized, the basic concept of composing organic music remains the same. The soil used to plant a tree may be capable of supporting a wide variety of plant species, but the basic elements in soil are required to grow the plant. In the same manner, the elements are used to create motives and the larger cornerstones of a composition.

Based on my definition of organic music, each element of the composition must play an essential role in how the work functions to behave organically. Music can exist, live, and function similarly to how an organism does. Ensure that most elements stem from some other aspect of the composition, whether it is the motive that creates a melody, the dynamic level that helps to identify a new section, or the timbre coupled with a specific harmony.

Furthermore, losing one element of the composition shouldn't result in a complete collapse of the work. Remove four consecutive notes from an eight-note melody, and the listener should still be able to identify the associated composition. When a composer constructs a piece where the motives that make up the melody are also present in the harmony and rhythm of the piece, then the music won't lose coherence even with the removal of a few elements. Consider a performance where a musician misses a few notes. The audience doesn't suddenly think the performer switched to a new composition, but the listeners often know when the performer makes a mistake. Let this concept sink in for a moment:

- When a performer makes a mistake and plays a wrong note, the audience may know, or at least sense, something is wrong.
- When a composer writes a section or note that doesn't make sense, the audience senses something is wrong.

Consider four complete works by the same composer with the melody removed from each composition. If a musician received the harvested melodies, it should still be possible to match the melody to the appropriate composition. If it's not possible, then the elements of the composition were too generic to be considered an organic work. Composers can think of this as a substitution test.

If you can substitute one melody with another melody and the piece still sounds fine, then the composition isn't unique enough to be considered organic.

The concept of substitution also applies to motives and, less commonly, cornerstones. Musicians should be able to identify the work that the melody belongs to by looking at the other elements in the composition and finding relationships between the melody and the rest of the work.

It bears repeating that by integrating elements throughout the piece, the composition should still be able to function on some level that is recognizable as belonging to the original even with missing parts.

164

Here is another example to make this point clear:
Organic music works in the same way as in a hypothetical traumatic situation where someone was to lose an arm. If this happened, presumably, others would still recognize the person. The person would be changed, but the basic features remain similar enough to be recognizable as belonging to the pre-accident individual.

This concept applies to small and large components equally. The orchestration is as vital as the soloist's melody to the overall cohesiveness of the entire work. The form is just as important as the motive that builds a composition. Start thinking about your music in terms of elements that create motives and infuse cornerstones, and you'll make significant progress as a composer and write pieces that make sense to the audience.

When Music Should Function Organically

One concept must be made very clear. There are many ways to compose music, and not all of them use organic techniques. However, learning to compose organic music is a sound method for learning to compose in general. Organic composition creates logical works, teaches the composer how to apply the different disciplines in music to a composition, and sets the stage for more advanced composing methods.

The goal of this philosophy of music composition is not to create ardent followers that use these principles to compose in "the only correct manner." The truth is that all of these techniques will only help a composer to ensure there is a good sense of variation, interest, and coherence in a musical work. Eventually, the composer must learn to compose entirely in their mind because that is the only way to be truly creative and to manipulate large-scale compositions in a truly artistic way. Notation programs or playing a piece on the piano can serve as a starting point, but there is nothing as fluid as the ability to compose entirely in one's mind.

Keep in mind that these principles work best with composers who also know theory, counterpoint, orchestration, and form. Organic principles are useful to extend and combine these theories for composers who want to think about the construction of music in a more creative way. As an educational tool, writing a composition that is created organically will help a composer to develop quickly and force them to consider the elements and cornerstones of a composition simultaneously.

When a composer develops the ability to compose organically, it's possible to integrate other techniques and systems:

- The Schillinger system has a wide variety of useful techniques, including permutations that can help composers learn to develop a composition.
- 12-Tone technique can help add highly dissonant, dense music to a work.
- Schenkerian analysis can make it easier to analyze the shape and effectiveness of a melody. But it does require some significant modifications and creativity to analyze modern works.

- Counterpoint can teach composers how chords developed from a historical context, and this can make it possible to understand why popular chord progressions like I-V-I exist and when it makes sense to forge new paths.

In an organic composition, melody, form, texture, harmony, and orchestration are not separated from each other and viewed independently. Though that is precisely how we teach music to composition students, we assign the student various techniques and concepts and ask them to find a way to integrate them on their own. This method proves useful for only the most talented, trained, and experienced composers. Most music students need additional instruction to learn how to integrate these disparate elements.

Writing organically serves as the bridge between the seemingly separate disciplines of counterpoint, orchestration, instrumentation, theory, form, and composition. When composers understand the concept of composing organic music, they can study individual subjects on their own merits and easily add additional techniques, systems, and theories to create a more fluid aesthetic of music composition. No system is perfect, but the concept of thinking organically about a musical work provides a framework to integrate all of the separate subjects and bring them together.

Creating a personal aesthetic is not easy, and it takes time and the proper guidance to learn how to accomplish it effectively. There is no quick fix for creating a work of art. Composers are competing with themselves and every other composer ever to live. To compete with the masters, a composer will need to become an expert in the craft and develop a flexible attitude towards the creation of new musical works. Ultimately though, good musical instincts need to be developed. I've found that an organic approach produces consistent and thorough results.

A Final Note About Composing

If you're not yet able to compose a musical work entirely in your mind, then you need to begin working on aural skills. Ear training techniques are essential to your development as a composer. It can take years to develop the ability to hear music entirely inside your mind, at which point, you can forego the notation programs and external instruments. Learning about music, listening to music, completing chord progressions by hand, copying music, and practicing daily ear training exercises are a few tricks that will help you to develop your inner ear.

This text is not designed to teach you how to compose music entirely in your mind, but I want you to know that it is possible. It is a goal you should strive for, and in the meantime, feel free to use your notation program or instrument to compose music. There are numerous techniques that I have developed to help composers, and myself, to learn to write music internally. Since the development of a robust inner ear is such a complex subject, it's a topic I deal with in-depth in the next volume of this series.

Practical and straightforward to apply exercises for developing the inner ear are available in the *Music Composition Technique Builder* text. One simple exercise you can begin trying right now is to imagine a single drone on one pitch. Then, try to add a second drone above that pitch. Move that drone up and down and get used to hearing an interval in your mind. I've developed several exercises that will help you improve your ear over a year, but you don't need to get the next book in the series to begin to develop your ear. Start by listening to as much music as you can internally, and you may find an incredible increase in your ability to hear music internally.

There is no quick fix or pill you can take to acquire an inner ear. It's essential to compose often and continue to develop your skill, but I wish I could give you a glimpse of what it is like to hear music entirely in your head. On the one hand, it's incredibly frustrating because you have to "listen" to the music repeatedly until you're able to notate it in the written form accurately. On the other, it's incredibly fulfilling to be able to hear a composition in full detail with a complete complement of inner parts that include elements, motives, and cornerstones. Your musical memory may be the most significant barrier to composing music entirely in your head. If you can't remember what you worked on the previous day, then the music will keep changing each time you go back to work. Of course, there are techniques you can use to deal with memory issues as well.

Developing your inner ear provides a good goal to work towards and to give you a preview of what the next text in this series aims to accomplish. *The Music Composition Technique Builder* gives you the exercises you need to develop your skills and improve your inner orchestra.

A composer must master their craft, trust their talent, and never stop pressing to create new works. Composition is a lifelong process in which no single person can ever learn all there is to know. Most importantly, don't forget to include the intuitive process in your musical works. Intuition and talent are the aspects of music that I have found cannot be taught, but you can refine and develop talent. Everything else a composer learns serves to hone their craft and forge their musical works into robust and effective musical compositions.

When you start to think of composing in three stages, you will begin to understand how to create more compelling compositions. While these stages often occur in succession, they don't have to follow a linear timeline. Inspiration and composing often work together simultaneously.

The first stage is inspiration: this is where you pull elements out of the air and combine them to create motives. Inspiration is a tiny part of composing, but it's also the one part that is difficult, if not impossible, to teach. Inspiration can be improved by listening to and studying a wide variety of music.

The second stage is composing: this is where you begin to expand your elements and motives to create phrases and embed elements into the more significant cornerstones of your music.

The third stage is editing: It's now time to look at your piece and put on your analysis hat. Evaluate your cornerstones to find areas that you could improve with your knowledge of the tenets and all of the experience you have at your disposal.

ADDITIONAL RESOURCES

- The Musical Core Lecture Series (2018)
- The Musical Core (2018)
- The Elements of Music Composition (2019)
- Music Composition Technique Builder (2019)
- The Craft of Music Composition (2020)
- The Art of Music Composition (2024)
- UreMusic.com and UreMusic.org

The Musical Core Lecture Series

The Musical Core is a public lecture series that takes students through the basics of music theory, and it also complements the online music theory and ear training course for students who purchase access. This is a good place to start to learn about music, how it developed, and gain insight into everything from note names to chords. A more user-friendly way to access the playlist is to visit KevinUre.com and click the YouTube link.

https://www.youtube.com/playlist?list=PLoSeDrmcZDEttC4666w2b79hoWoH7S-mN

The Musical Core (2019)

If you lack basic musicianship skills, this is the course for you. It provides ear training, basic music theory and exercises to help you develop the basic skills required to hone your craft. Through a combination of online courses, you can learn the basics that are required to complete additional theory courses. Information is available at themusicalcore.com, and it is published by Kendall Hunt Publishing Company. Visit TheMusicalCore.com or KendallHunt.com for more information.

The Elements of Music Composition (2018)

Composing Music Series Vol. I

The Elements of Music Composition serves as an introduction to the *Music Composition Technique Series*. It deals with the concept of coherence and comprehensibility in music so that you can begin to think about every component of a musical composition as related to the whole. This text provides the basis for a philosophy of music composition that does not demand strict theories of adherence to rules. This text details many of the concepts that I teach composers within private lessons, and it can serve as the basis for a music composition technique.

Music Composition Technique Builder (2019)

Composing Music Series Vol. II

This is the next text in the series after *The Elements of Music Composition*. The technique builder includes the resources and techniques that I use with my private students to develop their inner ear and learn how to conceptualize musical works entirely in their mind. Some of the exercises have also been developed while teaching university students basic musicianship skills, so these concepts are well-planned and organized. The techniques in this book have even led in an increase in students who have developed absolute pitch, although, that is not the goal of this text by any means.

The Craft of Music Composition (2022)

Composing Music Series (Volumes III-V)

For those who are interested in a more in-depth discussion of music theory topics, consider getting *The Craft of Music Composition* released in 2022. This series delves into harmony in a concise manner so that composers can integrate theory into their technique and move on with their composing lives. This text is also a great prep course for undergraduates, graduate review course, and reference for music theory instructors.

This course is based on undergraduate and graduate music theory courses I've taught, and it was developed while teaching at The University of Nevada, Las Vegas. Vol. III deals with counterpoint, Vol. IV addresses tonal harmony, and Vol. V addresses modern harmony. Additional volumes are planned for the future as well.

UreMusic.org and UreMusic.com

Students can read about all manner of music topics at UreMusic.org. Online music composition lessons are available through UreMusic.com. If you're interested in learning about additional composition books, courses, and lessons, you can visit the website at UreMusic.com.

Recommended Textbooks

I've also included a list of textbooks that I have recommended in this book. These books do not include edition numbers or publication dates since they tend to be updated frequently.

- *Analyzing Classical Form.* Caplin, William.
- *The Study of Orchestration.* Adler, Samuel.
- *Gradus ad Parnassum.* Fux, Joseph.
- *Theory of Harmony.* Schoenberg, Arnold.